Implement, Improve and Expand Your Statewide Longitudinal Data System

Wiley & SAS Business Series

The Wiley & SAS Business Series presents books that help senior-level managers with their critical management decisions.

Titles in the Wiley & SAS Business Series include:

Activity-Based Management for Financial Institutions: Driving Bottom-Line Results by Brent Bahnub

Big Data Analytics: Turning Big Data into Big Money by Frank Ohlhorst

Branded! How Retailers Engage Consumers with Social Media and Mobility by Bernie Brennan and Lori Schafer

Business Analytics for Customer Intelligence by Gert Laursen

Business Analytics for Managers: Taking Business Intelligence beyond Reporting by Gert Laursen and Jesper Thorlund

The Business Forecasting Deal: Exposing Bad Practices and Providing Practical Solutions by Michael Gilliland

Business Intelligence Success Factors: Tools for Aligning Your Business in the Global Economy by Olivia Parr Rud

CIO Best Practices: Enabling Strategic Value with Information Technology, Second Edition by Joe Stenzel

Connecting Organizational Silos: Taking Knowledge Flow Management to the Next Level with Social Media by Frank Leistner

Credit Risk Assessment: The New Lending System for Borrowers, Lenders, and Investors by Clark Abrahams and Mingyuan Zhang

Credit Risk Scorecards: Developing and Implementing Intelligent Credit Scoring by Naeem Siddiqi

The Data Asset: How Smart Companies Govern Their Data for Business Success by Tony Fisher

Delivering Business Analytics: Practical Guidelines for Best Practice by Evan Stubbs

Demand-Driven Forecasting: A Structured Approach to Forecasting, Second Edition by Charles Chase

Demand-Driven Inventory Optimization and Replenishment: Creating a More Efficient Supply Chain by Robert A. Davis

The Executive's Guide to Enterprise Social Media Strategy: How Social Networks Are Radically Transforming Your Business by David Thomas and Mike Barlow

Economic and Business Forecasting: Analyzing and Interpreting Econometric Results by John Silvia, Azhar Iqbal, Kaylyn Swankoski, Sarah Watt, and Sam Bullard

Executive's Guide to Solvency II by David Buckham, Jason Wahl, and Stuart Rose

Fair Lending Compliance: Intelligence and Implications for Credit Risk Management by Clark R. Abrahams and Mingyuan Zhang

Foreign Currency Financial Reporting from Euros to Yen to Yuan: A Guide to Fundamental Concepts and Practical Applications by Robert Rowan

Health Analytics: Gaining the Insights to Transform Health Care by Jason Burke

Human Capital Analytics: How to Harness the Potential of Your Organization's Greatest Asset by Gene Pease, Boyce Byerly, and Jac Fitz-enz

Information Revolution: Using the Information Evolution Model to Grow Your Business by Jim Davis, Gloria J. Miller, and Allan Russell

Manufacturing Best Practices: Optimizing Productivity and Product Quality by Bobby Hull

Marketing Automation: Practical Steps to More Effective Direct Marketing by Jeff LeSueur

Mastering Organizational Knowledge Flow: How to Make Knowledge Sharing Work by Frank Leistner

The New Know: Innovation Powered by Analytics by Thornton May

Performance Management: Integrating Strategy Execution, Methodologies, Risk, and Analytics by Gary Cokins

Predictive Business Analytics: Forward-Looking Capabilities to Improve Business Performance by Lawrence Maisel and Gary Cokins

Retail Analytics: The Secret Weapon by Emmett Cox

Social Network Analysis in Telecommunications by Carlos Andre Reis Pinheiro

Statistical Thinking: Improving Business Performance, Second Edition by Roger W. Hoerl and Ronald D. Snee

Taming the Big Data Tidal Wave: Finding Opportunities in Huge Data Streams with Advanced Analytics by Bill Franks

Too Big to Ignore: The Business Case for Big Data by Phil Simon

The Value of Business Analytics: Identifying the Path to Profitability by Evan Stubbs

Visual Six Sigma: Making Data Analysis Lean by Ian Cox, Marie A. Gaudard, Philip J. Ramsey, Mia L. Stephens, and Leo Wright

Win with Advanced Business Analytics: Creating Business Value from Your Data by Jean Paul Isson and Jesse Harriott

For more information on any of the above titles, please visit www.wiley.com.

Implement, Improve and Expand Your Statewide Longitudinal Data System

Creating a Culture of Data in Education

Jamie McQuiggan
Armistead W. Sapp III

WILEY

Library of Congress Cataloging-in-Publication Data:

McQuiggan, Jamie.
    Implement, improve and expand your statewide longitudinal data system :
creating a culture of data in education / Jamie McQuiggan, Armistead W. Sapp.
        pages cm. — (Wiley and SAS business series)
    ISBN 978-1-118-46677-3 (hardback); ISBN 978-1-118-84150-1 (ePDF);
ISBN 978-1-118-84154-9 (ePub); ISBN 978-1-118-84156-3 (oBook)
    1. Educational statistics—Computer programs. 2. Longitudinal method—Data
processing. I. Sapp, Armistead W. II. Title.
    LB2846.M3994 2014
    370.72'7—dc23

                                                        2013039757

This book is dedicated to the children. After all, it's really about them.

Contents

Foreword   xiii

Preface   xvii

Acknowledgments   xix

Chapter 1   How to Establish a Successful SLDS   1

What Is a Statewide Longitudinal Data System?   2

What an SLDS Can Do That Sneaker Net Cannot   4

What It Takes to Implement (or Improve) a Successful SLDS   9

Preview   13

Notes   15

Chapter 2   The SLDS Landscape   17

History of Longitudinal Data Systems   18

The State of SLDSs Today   23

Data Management Models   28

Conclusion   30

Notes   31

Chapter 3   Getting Started on Your SLDS   33

SLDS Planning and Preparation   35

Establish a Data Governance Board   35

Address Interoperability of the Data   38

Set Policies for Data Security and Student Privacy   41

Evaluate Current Systems and Make Connections   45

Make It Sustainable   50

Conclusion   53

Notes   54

Chapter 4 Data Management: Creating One Version of the Truth 57

What Is Master Data Management? 58

Incorporating MDM Principles in Your SLDS 60

Conclusion 75

Notes 75

Chapter 5 Florida Case Study: The Up- and Downside of Being the First 77

Florida's SLDS 78

Renovating What Exists Using Federal Grants 79

Conclusion 83

Notes 84

Chapter 6 Michigan Case Study: SLDS—a Tool for Reinventing the Economy 85

Michigan's SLDS: Moving Beyond Compliance 86

Career and College Ready Initiative: How Longitudinal Data Can Inform the Discussion 92

Conclusion 94

Notes 94

Chapter 7 North Carolina Case Study: New SLDS, Existing Partnerships 95

Stakeholders and the NC P20W System 96

The Vision 101

State Legislation Reinforcing SLDS 102

Conclusion 104

Notes 104

Chapter 8 Sharing Information with Others 105

Public Information Sharing: What Information Is the Public Entitled to and Interested In? 108

Policy Makers and State-Level Decision Makers: How Can Legislators Enable and Use Longitudinal Data? 109

Researchers: How Can States Leverage Researchers to Make the Longitudinal Data Answer Key Questions?   112

Establishing the Connection with Academia   114

Parents: What Longitudinal Data Do Parents Need, and How Will It Make a Difference?   118

Students: How Can Schools Provide Students with More Intuitive, Instant Access to Their Own Student Record Contextualized with Longitudinal Data?   122

Conclusion   124

Notes   124

Chapter 9   Using Data in Schools and Classrooms   127

Teachers   128

Administrators   134

The Teacher–Student Record Link   136

Conclusion   141

Notes   142

Chapter 10   Expanding Your SLDS: Adding Out-of-School Time and Health-Care Data   145

Collective Impact: The Longitudinal Data Connection   148

OST: What Happens When They're Not in School?   149

Health-Care Data   153

How to Facilitate Collective Impact Initiatives   157

Conclusion   160

Notes   161

Chapter 11   A Culture of Data: Using Longitudinal Data to Solve Big Problems   163

Creating a Culture of Data   164

Data-Driven Decision Tools   171

Response to Intervention (RTI)   172

Early Warning Systems   177

Conclusion   180

Notes   181

Chapter 12   It's Not about the Data   185

Ways to Sustain the System   188

Conclusion   193

Notes   194

About the Authors   195

Index   197

Foreword

How do today's educators teach the necessary skills for tomorrow's skilled workforce? How do we find and reward effective teachers? How do we maximize the diminishing resources available to schools to make them more successful? These are just a few of the pressing and difficult questions facing our educational system today.

Although I am not an educator, I have been privileged to be directly involved in more facets of the educational process than most business leaders, as a student, professor, parent and developer of educational software. On a personal level, my early years as a student were shaped by a high school teacher who encouraged me to pursue science. And shortly after earning my Ph.D. in statistics and teaching the subject at the graduate level, my career was again influenced by my department head and other university leaders, who encouraged several of us to continue our work outside the university, as entrepreneurs. We took their advice and started a company called SAS.

As SAS grew, so too did our need for highly qualified knowledge workers. We needed people who could quickly adapt our software to new computer processors and new architectures, and required graduates with STEM (science, technology, engineering and math) skills and a strong education. By the 1990s, we realized that there was a problem: The supply of highly specialized workers coming out of the U.S. educational system was not enough to meet the demand. After a closer look, we were shocked to see that the problem was not at the graduate or undergraduate level but was in high school and even in middle school. The national high school dropout rate was a staggering 30 percent. Not only did that number vary from state to state (and from school district to school district), there was also no national standard for concepts such as data collection, reporting or calculating cohort four-year dropout rates. In fact, this data issue prevented us from even having a true national dropout rate, as different schools and districts classify dropouts differently.

The lack of qualified, educated workers that SAS noticed is corroborated as the United States continues to straggle in global educational rankings. In 2012, the United States was 17th in reading, 26th in math and 21st in science, according to the Programme for International Student Assessment (PISA) study. Not only do the PISA findings highlight poor U.S. academic performance, but they also intensify the need for U.S. educators to better measure and report on student progress and knowledge levels. These issues aren't going away, and they impact our economy.

Success in school, specifically graduating from high school and attending college, is more important than ever in preparing students for success in life. A high school and college education will provide students with more opportunities in the knowledge economy. In the past, a high school education or less still allowed for students to get a job in a factory or trade and do well if they were willing to work hard. Now, better education has become a necessity for surviving in the knowledge economy and is a strong determining factor for socioeconomic success. The jobs of today and tomorrow are increasingly requiring broad education rather than specialized training. The knowledge economy demands at least a high school diploma to certify that the new class of workers is ready to jump into well-paid and increasingly technical jobs. And as a society, it behooves us to prepare our students to graduate and rise to this challenge, to succeed in the knowledge economy. As a country, we are failing academically and failing to provide the knowledge workers that companies like SAS depend on.

How can school systems, faced with diminishing resources, unsatisfactory results and increased stakes address these challenges to give America's youth the education they need to succeed in the future?

There is one very powerful, underutilized tool in the educational tool box: data. Having organized, analyzed and up-to-date data available to decision makers, practitioners and customers is fundamental to revolutionizing the way they do business. Having data as the central support for organizational operations is the new normal for many sectors; it is no longer "nice to have" but is absolutely invaluable to day-to-day operations. It should be the norm for our national educational system as well.

Many administrators of educational systems see an efficient and connected data system like a statewide longitudinal data system (SLDS) as a challenge—it'd be great, but not worth the time and resources to set it up. They see it as secondary to providing education to their students, to managing their employees, tracking and reporting test scores, increasing their graduation rates and fighting budget cuts. In fact, an SLDS can provide the data necessary to drive better decisions and provide real-time feedback, have an impact on each of the aforementioned areas and change what administrators know and how they make their decisions. States that delay or ignore this technological game changer are thus missing the point entirely. Without investment in an interconnected, longitudinal data structure, those states will invariably fall further behind in the future. To continue to meet the growing (and changing) demands, to make data-supported decisions and better utilize resources and talent and to enable smarter reforms, an information-driven infrastructure is vital. Data is the key.

Schools have been slow to change the way they view data, and there are many reasons this change has come about slowly. It's ironic, though, that the main reason for the delay—money—is also a primary benefit of a functional SLDS. Educational systems are influenced by different forces than those currently revolutionizing business sectors, which have to undertake rapid development of their information management structures to succeed. However, education also has a lot at stake; real opportunity exists, at high levels of government funding, to fundamentally restructure the way education administrators store and organize their data and, indeed, the way they value and use that data to inform their work.

The need for highly skilled knowledge workers is growing, and we anticipate that this trend will continue. SLDSs offer the opportunity to gain more insight into the educational system, turning information into knowledge and changing the way education does business. As a business leader and employer of knowledge workers, I believe that this book is an important step in that direction.

Dr. Jim Goodnight, Ph.D.
Chief Executive Officer, SAS

Preface

We set out to write this book with the intention of helping states maximize their *statewide longitudinal data systems* (SLDSs) and create an enduring culture of data in schools. It is our hope that this book will help in furthering the discussion for states still considering an SLDS and will help states that have implemented a first-generation SLDS think about how to improve and expand their systems to deliver on the promise of longitudinal data.

This book covers most of the steps necessary to implement or improve your SLDS, outlining areas for growth and expansion. We've found that about 80 percent of the work of implementing an SLDS lies in simply reaching *agreement of what the SLDS is:* what data it will contain, what questions it needs to answer, and how that data will be accessed and shared by the various stakeholders in the education and workforce sectors. Once states work out the data governance of the system and use, implementation is fairly simple.

The resource that can be created from years and years of data is immense. Think about when you watch a documentary on Netflix about the *Titanic.* After you watch it and tell Netflix you enjoyed it, Netflix can recommend several documentaries that other users like you enjoyed, based on your rating and viewing history. The more data the recommendation engine has, the better it is at recommending what you'll enjoy next. Now, imagine you're an elementary student with ADHD and your teachers have tried several interventions with no success. What if your teachers could access data on other students like you, immediately seeing which interventions worked to teach them about photosynthesis, or how to cross-multiply? This sort of targeted recommendation system exists; SLDS gives systems like these the historical data they need to be relevant to today's educational problems.

Creating a *culture of data* is the necessary ideological shift to accompany any SLDS implementation. A culture of data is one where best practices in the classroom and in the management of schools and districts are chosen based on data. Ideally, everyone in the educational system—from state-level administrators and teachers to students and parents—is taught how to include data in their decision making. It's a huge shift, but one that can revolutionize the educational system.

The authors work at SAS Institute and have worked with all aspects of implementing SLDSs, from assisting in grant writing, to implementing new systems as well as helping to fix and update systems that were not doing what the state expected. SAS is a worldwide leader in business intelligence software, and has long advocated the benefits of data in decision making. We find the inclusion of data-driven decision making into education to be logical and exciting.

Acknowledgments

This book has two coauthors and a long list of folks who helped. Making connections and facilitating interviews, giving time in reviewing what we wrote and sharing their expertise and insight, these folks were an integral part in the writing and completion of this book and we offer our sincere thanks.

Thanks go to Emily Baranello for her passionate help at every stage of the writing of this book. We also wish to thank Jim and Ann Goodnight for their support of education and allowing us the time to work with many different parts of the education system in the United States.

For the graphics and creative illustrations, we thank the SAS BIRD Graphic Divas, Tammi Kay George and Lisa Morton.

Big thanks go to our colleagues at SAS for helping to make connections with educators, administrators and experts, and supporting our efforts in writing this book: Elizabeth Ceranowski, Christine Bevan, Bob Tschudi, Colleen Jenkins, Missy Poynter, Rob Harper, Courtney Verska, Kristin McCown, Barbara Flannery, Keli Lloyd, Michael Drutar, Liz Riley-Young, Chris Ricciardi, Ottis Cowper and Scott McQuiggan.

We thank the SAS Publishing team for their expert guidance through the process of writing our first book: Stacey Hamilton, Shelley Sessoms and Julie Platt. A special thank-you to the SAS Library team for their help in researching: Jennifer Evans, Elaine Teague, Karissa Wrenn and Julia Legeros.

We had an amazing set of reviewers who were candid with their feedback and whose input ultimately made this a better book. Thank you, Karl Pond, Mohamed Dirir and Georgia Mariani.

We conducted many interviews and had many conversations with subject-matter experts and educators. While this is not a comprehensive list, we'd like to thank Tom Howell, Kit Goodner, Gene Kovacs,

Saundra Williams, Steven Hopper, Amy Wilkinson, Ada Lopez, Sylvia Allen, Deveial Foster, Karen Pittman, Paul Evensen, Elizabeth Laird (DQC), Emily Anthony (NCES), Sean Mulvenon, Charlene Swanson and Baron Rodriguez.

CHAPTER 1

How to Establish
a Successful SLDS

Larry and Helen work in the project office for the governor. Larry is a data analyst and Helen is a technologist, and, as a team of two, they're responsible for fulfilling information requests from various parties across the state. They receive a request from the state legislature. The state's elementary schools have been the benefi- ciaries of a generous donation from a private foundation to fund a new program designed to improve their Instructional Improvement Systems (IIS), and the two-year funding period is coming to a close. The state legislature wants to know if the program has worked and if its continuation should be funded. They want to know if the IIS program shows measurable gains among students who participated.

In the same state, at Ashley Elementary, John is a new student in Mrs. Fraser's third-grade class. He is reading below grade level, and Mrs. Fraser wants to help him. She is curious as to what John's previous schools have tried to remediate his needs. She needs this information quickly, so time isn't lost in addressing John's pressing need. Before he's compelled to repeat third grade or gets pushed into alternative education, Mrs. Fraser is anxious to pick up where previous teachers have left off to improve John's reading.

The governor wants to begin a task force to reduce the number of high school dropouts in the state. She asks the state's Department of Education to supply the following information to provide the backbone for an early warning system that alerts educators when kids show certain characteristics. What are the characteristics of high school dropouts? Are there early predictors schools could find in elementary or middle school to better identify at-risk individuals? Do these predictors change in different geographic areas or among different demographic populations?

All of these examples are largely changed by the availability of longitudinal data, those data that provide the same measure over time. Without a comprehensive state system, the requestors of data will collect the data, collate them and assemble them in a way that makes sense and is usable. And the process can take several weeks, if it's even possible to collect all of the information. This system, Sneaker Net, has prevailed over the past decade. It is inefficient and has low levels of accuracy and security. If the state had an SLDS (statewide longitudinal data system), answering these requests would be much simpler, even instantaneous. Larry and Helen transition to maintaining the data, queries and systems, with much less legwork in obtaining the data from each agency. The validity of each data set is higher, as there is less room for human error.

This chapter will provide a foundation for the rest of the book: defining an SLDS, enumerating the benefits and selling points of these systems to convince those who aren't quite sure if it's worth the effort, and detailing how to establish new systems or improve existing ones to make them more efficient. We'll refer to the previous examples throughout the book to illustrate features and benefits as they pertain to various stakeholders and users of the system.

WHAT IS A STATEWIDE LONGITUDINAL DATA SYSTEM?

Siloed data is a pervasive issue among educational data. Many educational systems are housed within different agencies, tracking student data and not communicating. Housing data in siloed and disparate systems poses many problems for states in using data to solve issues (some of which are enumerated at the beginning of this chapter).

Uniting these systems that house student data is a prime way to make these data useful. *Statewide longitudinal data systems* (SLDSs) track student data from preschool through college and workforce across the state. The federal government is encouraging states to develop and implement SLDSs to track and analyze their data. Initiatives like the America COMPETES Act, the No Child Left Behind Act, the American Recovery and Reinvestment Act, the Race to the Top program and various grant programs provide direct incentive to states that are at the leading edge in this enterprise. The Data Quality Campaign, a national advocate for longitudinal data usage and availability, found that currently, every state in the country is at some point in the process of developing an SLDS, some in the very early stages and some near completion.[1] Each state has longitudinal data. States are at varying points in maximizing the potential that SLDSs have to offer, and many are not yet using the data in substantially new and meaningful ways. States seem to be on board with the idea of an SLDS in theory, and the next key step is to empower states, educators and legislators to use and analyze the data to aid in providing education to students. It's time to put the data to work.

The defining characteristics of a statewide longitudinal data system are important to note, as the concepts that follow will depend upon a common understanding of the purported outcome.

- An SLDS tracks and maintains student- and staff-level data across the whole state (not simply district-wide or county-wide).
- An SLDS links these data across entities and over time, providing a robust and complete academic history for each student, as well as aggregated data about subgroups of students.
- An SLDS makes these data available to researchers and other educational agencies for analysis and reporting.[2]
- An SLDS provides current data to stakeholders in a secure manner.

Simply having data or a database with multiple contributing sources does not mean that an agency has a longitudinal data system. The key characteristic, as contrasted to the prevailing data storing and reporting methods still used in some states, is the ability to see student-level data over time and to use these data in the aggregate to spot trends and improve the education system.

Any type of SLDS will involve the assigning of a *unique identifier* (UID) to each student, as the student's Social Security number is not an acceptable way to identify a student. This UID is the key data value by which records are merged and integrated on all SLDSs, essentially enabling the connection between P–12 data and other state agencies. Adoption of a UID system by all parties, or a bridge to allow for matching on some other data field, is the first step toward a unified data system. Having a UID that follows the student as he moves to a different school, graduates or drops out, and enters the workforce enables the educational system to have easy access to rich data it has never had before.

One way to visualize the contrast between traditional educational databases and an SLDS is to think in terms of photography. Previous data-tracking methods consisted of snapshots of the child during standardized tests and report card grades, with gaps in between. An SLDS, then, is a video recording of each child from the day he sets foot in the public education system until he graduates college and enters the workforce. With much more footage (data) for each student, educators could note subtle changes that wouldn't have otherwise been obvious.[3]

WHAT AN SLDS CAN DO THAT SNEAKER NET CANNOT

An SLDS is a useful and important tool in performing existing reporting tasks more efficiently as well as using data to identify trends and make policy changes. In the examples from this chapter, an SLDS would give each party the ability to quickly and accurately get the answers they're seeking.

Establishing an SLDS is no small feat. It requires consensus among groups who are often unaccustomed to working together and sharing data, as well as changes in format and processes to ensure the data are interoperable and secure. And, perhaps most important, a successful SLDS implementation will require a culture shift in how the state's educational system as a whole views data as integral to its continued value and use. There are many substantial benefits to states that establish an SLDS that far outweigh the potential difficulties and obstacles to the effort. This list of benefits is designed to give a picture of what can be gained from a robust and comprehensive SLDS project.

Asking Questions and Getting Timely Answers

Simply put, the SLDS allows for streamlined question asking and answering. Storing vast amounts of longitudinal data allows the ability to ask questions across time, not just over the 1–2 years that most transactional systems allow. This is tremendously valuable in getting a full picture of the child's education, spotting issues and opportunities. It can be an ongoing information source, not only when information is officially requested (as in our examples). An SLDS provides another valuable asset that a simple database cannot: timely answers. In addition to including larger amounts of data, teachers and administrators are able to get near-real-time answers to questions. In past models, data queried are several months—if not years—old, yielding results that don't give administrators the opportunity to act. An SLDS allows for quick results drawn from updated information. The primary benefit to having updated information is the ability to act in a timely fashion. Further, quality and updated data availability will encourage the culture shift to asking deep and probing questions for the betterment of the education system.

Additionally, the ability to receive quick and accurate answers enables smarter reform. Being able to know if a reform initiative is working in a timely manner can influence its continued funding, as in the case of the state legislature asking about the effectiveness of the elementary reading program in our example. Even more important, research can become the backbone for new initiatives, driving policy rather than simply supporting it. Longitudinal data are essential to gauging the need for change: what sort of change to make to address the problem and evaluation of whether certain reforms are working. As it stands now and in old Sneaker Net systems, most decisions are being made on anecdotal hunches, a far cry from the data-driven decisions a comprehensive SLDS enables. Giving policy makers the ability to ask questions and receive an immediate answer with up-to-date data is one of the most promising, game-changing features of an SLDS.

Ultimately, linking disparate data sources also leads to the ability to learn new things about the data, which simply isn't feasible with siloed data. As needs evolve and the complexity of research questions grows, an SLDS can accommodate this. You can ask questions you didn't know you wanted to ask, and as long as the data are collected and stored, you can get the answer. SLDSs open new doors, allowing new connections to be explored.

Data-Driven Decisions That Can Impact Student Outcomes in Real Time

SLDSs enable proactive, preventative measures to be taken to correct the course of students on the wrong track. In the example of the governor's task force to lower the high school dropout rate at the beginning of the chapter, longitudinal data are an integral part of implementing the early warning system and doing the research to create it. Past models relied more on reactive action occurring after the fact. For instance, a student has dropped out of high school, so his record is evaluated and administrators might try to figure out where he got off the path to success. With an SLDS, it is easy to track dropout factors, and receiving alerts in a timely fashion affords administrators the opportunity for early intervention and the possibility to *prevent* a dropout from occurring. Research suggests that "failing grades in reading or math, poor behavior, being over age for grade, having a low grade 9 grade-point average, failing grade 9 or having a record of frequent transfers" are all factors that could flag a student as someone who might be more likely to drop out.[4] Students who show these signs could be provided early intervention and perhaps their course could be reversed if these risk factors were flagged in time for action to be taken. *Response to intervention* and *early warning systems* accomplish this, showing how the data supplied by an SLDS might change the way education is given to students to prevent negative outcomes. These systems are detailed in Chapter 11. Providing more information in a uniform format facilitates this new culture of research possibilities.[5]

Another important facet of facilitating data-driven decisions is providing data to teachers in the classroom. In an SLDS, comprehensive student-level data are stored on the student record and can be provided to teachers. When a child moves from one grade to the next, teachers can be provided with more timely information than ever before about the child's past grades, behaviors, test scores and risk factors. Before the school year even begins, a teacher has a window into each child's specific needs. Rather than solving issues as they arise, teachers can proactively address student needs, giving extra attention to areas of weakness or concern or creating a more challenging plan for students with high aptitude. In our example, Mrs. Fraser would see on John's record which interventions were used to improve his reading skills, enabling more targeted methods. And, in turn, the interventions she tries with John will be included on his record for future reference.

More Accurate and Effective Reporting

The implementation of an SLDS provides state and local educational administrators a vehicle for timely and accurate reporting with a reduction of effort. The integration of data from multiple sources to ensure that the reports are accurate reduces the burden of governmental reporting.

State and local educational agencies have the burden of many mandated state and federal reports. Having an interoperable set of data in an updated and standardized format allows for more efficient, and where possible, automated querying of data. This substantially cuts the amount of time and resources needed for recurring and required reports. A unified system and data standard among all educational agencies in the state further reduces data entry redundancies, and therein, errors. Take the example of the high school dropout task force. Even getting a true number of high school dropouts across the state is problematic, as the system is fraught with differing definitions and classifications of what constitutes a *dropout*.[6] Issues relating to classification of special cases (i.e., a student who leaves high school to enter college early is sometimes classified as a dropout) would be addressed at the outset of the establishment of an SLDS, providing states and local educational agencies (LEAs) with the opportunity to have an accurate picture of their dropout rate. Thus, for Larry and Helen to provide the numbers to the requesters, it would take far less time and be more accurate. In this way, an SLDS allows for more educational agency time and energy to be put toward analyzing data and helping students.

New Connections and Increased Collaboration

Fundamentally, an SLDS links systems that are not connected. While this is certainly a difficult process, it leads to less duplication of effort and more accuracy and security for the data. In any educational system, be it a local district or an entire state, there are multiple databases to be included in an SLDS, often with different data sets and different purposes for existence. One group might track student test scores, another student attendance records, and another student special needs. It is essential in the establishment of an SLDS that these systems "speak the same language" and map to the same data standard (most commonly, the *Common Education Data Standards [CEDS]*). Systems that are unable to meet the standard mandated by the Governance body for the SLDS cannot integrate to the system. Providing a database with multiple sourcing and interoperable data is essential in meeting the needs of users going forward into the culture of data-driven decision making. To answer any of the above example questions would involve dozens of individual requests to local agencies and queries to state databases. It would further involve deduplication and collation of the information to make it meaningful, all of which are time consuming and prone to human error. In short, without an SLDS, these sorts of insightful research questions are simply not feasible.

Having a *statewide* LDS can save time and money for LEAs that want this level of technology but can't fund it in its entirety at the local level. Fostering collaboration on the state level will free up LEA time, give the LDS a higher level of investment and buy-in and prevent the LEA from having to go it alone. "With a statewide LDS project, states should think of districts as partners, rather than as customers. As such, the LDS should be conceptualized and developed not as something that districts simply need to comply with, but as a valuable tool that will benefit both the state and the district."[7]

A Measure for Educational Effectiveness

A functioning SLDS system, ultimately, is a tool that provides accurate and important insights about a state's overall effectiveness—its success in educating students, effectiveness of its teachers, and progress in its schools, district, programs and initiatives. Data showing ineffective programs or schools can have impact on funding decisions. What is at stake when we're discussing the implementation of an SLDS is the future of education, fueled by data-driven decisions.

Further, the ability to tie student records to the teachers of record offers another opportunity for insight. The ability to spot excellent and effective teachers encourages wider adoption of their techniques, and rewarding their efforts should encourage a culture of excellence. On the other end of this spectrum, being able to identify ineffective teachers and provide remediation provides the opportunity for reinforcement of a culture of excellence. *Teacher–student* longitudinal data would encourage teacher preparation programs to monitor the success or weakness of teachers and adjust their programs to be more effective.

WHAT IT TAKES TO IMPLEMENT (OR IMPROVE) A SUCCESSFUL SLDS

States are at various points in their SLDS development and implementation. Even systems that have been functional for years are trying to make improvements to make their systems more efficient and modern. How do states get to the point where they can make data-driven decisions and improve educational outcomes? What are the things they can do as they design and implement systems to promote long-term success? There are a few key areas that should be focused on when strategic decisions are being made for design and improvement of SLDSs, as illustrated in Figure 1.1. States need to improve *processes, technology* and *leadership* surrounding their SLDSs and data management to get to the next level.

Processes

Setting up an SLDS typically takes several years of planning, executing and negotiations between stakeholders on how to get the data compatible and in a common place to be shared and accessed. Through these exercises, processes will be established to enable consistent and easy operation of the SLDS in common, predictable scenarios. While the method of establishing the SLDS can feel drawn out and tedious at

Figure 1.1 Implementing or Improving a Successful SLDS

times, if done thoroughly, it should establish guidelines for access, privacy and data-quality processes. Establishing a uniform way for these recurring actions to be handled is essential.

It is important to establish processes for data security and student privacy. This is a common concern among stakeholders, as they can vouch for their own security practices within their own system but are unsure of how others treat student data. And, sharing data often means more risk of disclosure. While this is always a possibility, a good SLDS with strong processes and policies will almost definitely be more secure than the siloed systems of today. Richard Culatta of the U.S. Department of Education notes that "there are times where using technology carefully can actually help us improve privacy and security."[8] To this point, a unified data system means that all agencies are on the same page, using an agreed-upon high standard of security for student data. It will outline and enable secure sharing, a vast improvement over siloed systems' current processes. Culatta mentions one example of how a student record travels from one school to another if the student moves. Typically, the record is printed out, mailed and reentered, leaving several opportunities for it to be lost, to be seen by unauthorized eyes or for errors to be made in entering the data. Having a way to share these records using the data system seamlessly safeguards all parties and makes for a more secure system.

To have a successful SLDS, there must be processes for sharing data with the larger database, and processes for authorized uses to access the data. These processes will all be enumerated in the planning stage and be changed with group consensus, but having an agreed-upon process is crucial to a functional SLDS. And finally, a process for data quality will be created and instituted, giving all the users faith in the validity of data used from other agencies. To be a successful SLDS, users must trust that the output is valid and can be relied upon. Data quality procedures will ensure the continuing compatibility of data and the consistency of data across sources.

Technology

Though an SLDS is not solely a technical project and should have representation from all areas of educational agencies involved in its implementation, the technical component of the project can't be ignored. There are definite system requirements that must be satisfied to make a functional and usable system that performs as the users' desire. The technology component includes hardware, software and system design. It is important to understand how much data the system will need to manage, how much will be added yearly and how the system will be used. All of these data points will inform the hardware, software and system design.

It is hard to overstate how important it is to have a system with good design. Users have become accustomed to highly usable and intuitive cloud-based web applications, such as iTunes and Gmail; data systems should strive to meet this level of simplicity and usability. If the system is usable, intuitive and gives the users information they need easily, it will be accessed and utilized more often. Design SLDSs with dashboards and end-user input. Don't simply design a system and use professional development time to train users. While training on a new system is, of course, necessary, it shouldn't be the only way that a new user can figure out the system. Spend time in the development and design of the SLDS. Meet with end users to have them test and try the design. Using their input and feedback will ensure that the end result will be a functional and useful system that can be accessed and understood. Good design will enable high levels of use.

Make sure the software can accomplish all it needs to and that it is powerful enough to enable analytics, reporting and sharing in the high volumes that an SLDS should accommodate. The software should be powerful enough to grow as your need for analysis and information grows, facilitating data management and enabling reporting systems to function. Some software solutions can address all of these needs, while others would necessitate a more piecemeal solution, combining several systems. And, ensure the hardware can host the large data sets that will live on an SLDS. Millions of student records, and over time those numbers will only grow, should be accommodated on the SLDS.

Leadership

Ultimately, an SLDS can't be a successful initiative and investment if all levels of educational data agencies in the state are not on board in creating a culture of data. This means continually reinforcing the benefits to stakeholders and communicating regularly to share status, priorities and changes. Keeping the team engaged, informed and committed is essential to maintaining buy-in at all levels. Intelligent and enthusiastic leadership is a must-have for any SLDS project.

The *data governance committee*, assembled with representation from all stakeholder groups and educational agencies, will largely set the tone for the project and provide leadership on the project. As influencers within their agencies, they can share the news with their colleagues, and can help steer the project in positive directions. Setting up Governance is discussed in Chapter 3.

To further reinforce the importance of longitudinal data, administrators must be invested in data to drive decisions. When a change is proposed, data must be demanded to support the new proposal. Showing, rather than simply telling, that data-driven decisions are the new normal is a key way to prove the game has shifted in educational data. Further, using data to support their evaluations of teachers in the school and encouraging use of data to make classroom decisions are key administrator responsibilities in shifting the culture of the school to a more data-centric one.

Involved, informed and passionate leadership is also vital to maintain the political will to keep the SLDS project moving and funded. Make no mistake—creating and maintaining an SLDS is an arduous task but one that is worth the investment. Make sure that in the early stages these leaders are chosen wisely.

To establish or improve your SLDS, it's important to consider each of the three areas for development and attention: processes, technology and leadership. Addressing these areas enables your system to grow over time and adapt to future changes in needs. How do you design a system that meets the needs of your state and the various interests at different levels within the education system, and within the budget available? This book will tackle these logistical issues, tell the stories of several unique SLDSs in different states and outline a roadmap for SLDS growth and data use.

PREVIEW

Though for many readers the situations described at the beginning of the chapter and the roadblocks they highlight are a reality, we write this book to provide a roadmap for successful implementation and expansion of an SLDS to help positively change the landscape of education in the United States. Providing schools, administrators and educational agencies on all levels with better data and the power to use the data for improvement is the ultimate vision for SLDSs.

We hope to provide background and guidance for new SLDSs, as well as a resource for existing SLDSs that are aiming to enhance certain aspects of their systems. Throughout the book, we discuss the concept of a culture of data, and how to instill it at all levels of the educational data pipeline.

In Chapter 2, we discuss the SLDS landscape, providing a background in student data management and common database architectures. An overview of the current state of SLDSs nationwide will be included, as well as common challenges SLDSs face.

Chapter 3 details the planning process, including best practices regarding data governance, standards and privacy. In addition, we will discuss CEDS and the importance of data interoperability standards.

Chapter 4 provides an in-depth discussion of data management practices and database architecture, a key decision for each state to make in designing its SLDS. We provide explanations on master data management and metadata management, as well as compare and contrast the two primary architectures for SLDSs: centralized data warehouse and federated data system.

Chapters 5–7 include three case studies, describing states that provide exemplary models in SLDS implementation and practice. Each case study provides details about what makes the state's SLDS unique and the challenges it faces. Michigan's, North Carolina's and Florida's SLDSs are featured.

Chapters 8 and 9 outline the importance of sharing data with educators and other individuals who are entitled to have access to student and educational data. Researchers, policy makers, parents, students and administrators are discussed as parties who should be included in the SLDS. Each has something to gain from the data in the SLDS, which can impact their roles significantly.

Chapter 10 makes the case for including out-of-school time and health-care data in the SLDS in order to give a fuller picture of the student. These nonacademic factors can impact a student's success in school, and including them in the data set gives educators a chance to better understand and address these outside factors. Additionally, as more states get their SLDSs established and functional with educational data, the shift to focusing on expansion will mean more states will move to incorporate data from additional sources that give a fuller picture of the student.

Chapter 11 describes how the culture of data built around longitudinal data used can solve many of the difficult problems plaguing our educational system. Leadership and the implementation of several key tools and applications that work within the SLDS enable more proactive data use. Using response to intervention programs becomes more intelligent with shared longitudinal data, and early warning systems provide useful alerts using the SLDS, enabling real-time intervention.

Finally, Chapter 12 revisits how the examples we offered at the beginning of this chapter are substantially changed with access to longitudinal data. We also discuss how to promote accountability, data access and institutional change using the SLDS.

NOTES

1. Data Quality Campaign, *Data Quality Campaign*, December 2011, http://dataquali tycampaign.org/files/DFA2011%20Mini%20report%20findings%20Dec1.pdf (accessed January 6, 2012).
2. National Forum on Educational Statistics, *Traveling Through Time: The Forum Guide to Longitudinal Data Systems. Book 1 of 4: What Is an LDS?* (Alexandria, VA: ED Publishers, 2010), http://nces.ed.gov/pubsearch/pubsinfo.asp?pubid=2010805.
3. Ibid.
4. Robert M. Hauser and Judith Anderson Koenig, *High School Dropout, Graduation and Completion Rates: Better Data, Better Measures, Better Decisions* (Washington, DC: National Academies Press, 2011).
5. National Forum on Educational Statistics, *Traveling Through Time*.
6. Hauser and Koenig, *High School Dropout, Graduation and Completion Rates*.
7. National Forum on Educational Statistics, *Traveling Through Time*.
8. Richard Culatta, "Is Student Data Education's Next Frontier?" SXSWedu Conference, Austin, TX, March 2013.

CHAPTER 2

The SLDS Landscape

Today's educational landscape is demanding; we're living in a climate where expectations are higher than they've ever been before. As a country, we've set the lofty goal of having every child graduate from high school ready for college or the knowledge economy. And, indeed, with good, high-paying jobs increasingly demanding a college (or higher) education, a high school degree is truly necessary for a job in the knowledge economy. Widespread budget cuts are giving fewer resources to state educational agencies (SEAs) and local educational agencies (LEAs), yet all are still expected to improve efficiency, improve system performance, improve student outcomes and increase transparency. How can LEAs and SEAs face the increasing challenges and overcome them to produce more successes than ever before? In a word: data. The Data Quality Campaign's (DQC) founder and executive director Aimee Guidera noted, "We will never meet any of these goals, never mind all of these goals, unless we change the conversation to how are we going to use data effectively to meet them."[1]

Establishing an SLDS (statewide longitudinal data system) poses several hurdles for states. Implementation of an SLDS requires that data be shared across systems that previously weren't required to share data. This causes many logistical challenges, requiring changes in technological capabilities and increased or reallocated resources. Institutional change can come slowly. Educational data are some of the most segregated and fractured data in the world. In one school system, there are often separate data systems for the lunchroom data, the library data, the online gradebook, the end-of-grade test results and attendance record. So, if a child receives a subsidized lunch, has a late library book, misses many days of school and gets poor grades, all of these data points are not on the same record and can't be easily used to paint a whole picture of what's happening in the child's life. There are many interoperability challenges in enabling these systems to share data among themselves.

Further, in the past, data provided by educational agencies have often been used to highlight failings and, at times, punish, rather than be analyzed to illuminate wide trends and advise future actions. Skepticism to the intentions and uses of shared data remains among data-stewards and the public when implementing an SLDS. When coupled with the ever-present budget cuts faced almost across the board by school districts everywhere, it's easy to push the establishment of an SLDS down on the priority list. Indeed, to fully realize the potential of SLDSs, state educational agencies must facilitate a culture shift to one where data are seen as a tool rather than a chore, one that will enable more efficient time usage and better decisions that will ultimately save the state educational systems money. Data use has changed many other industries in this way; it's time for it to revolutionize the way the education system is operated.

HISTORY OF LONGITUDINAL DATA SYSTEMS

Over its short history, longitudinal data systems have grown from being simply about compliance with government mandated reporting to showing accountability and evaluation to today's focus on continuous improvement. SLDSs offer the ability to provide near-real-time data that affect a state's or district's actions and improve student outcomes.

The beginnings of the data systems that are part of today's longitudinal data systems mostly grew out of requirements from various government levels. They didn't grow in an orderly fashion and the result was a rather disconnected and disorganized system. The goal was not to drive student achievement and improve education, but rather to comply with reporting regulations that were thrust upon educational agencies as a condition to receive government funding.[2] Initiatives like the National Assessment for Educational Progress (NAEP) in 1971 and the National Longitudinal Studies in 1972 test children nationwide to show trends and progress. These cross-sectional data points show valuable information, but it is not as rich as longitudinal data.[3]

A new era in educational data was ushered in during the 1990s. States and schools moved to recognize an accountability model as the driving force behind their data collection and reporting. As a result there was a huge uptick in the amount of student data being tracked and reported. Being able to survey several years of data to see if a program worked was now possible. Government and philanthropic organizations began to demand these results to prove the money they had given was achieving its intended purposes, resulting in more accountability from educational agencies. Though this step was a great move forward in educational data, it still only offered a rearview-mirror perspective on which policies and actions worked or did not work; it did not offer the chance to change course and create a different outcome. By the time the data were collected and analyzed, the students were out of the classroom and their outcomes unchangeable.[4]

The current era of educational data affords the ability to offer continuous improvement or, essentially, the ability to look out the front window and see where the agency is heading and what factors might come into play and make decisions that can affect near-real-time outcomes. The data being surveyed are on current students and, in certain situations, can be acted upon to improve those student outcomes.[5] The vision for SLDSs is to increase schools' and SEAs' capacity to make real-time proactive decisions and continue to positively impact the educational system with data-driven decision making, continuing down the path of continuous improvement.

The United States Department of Education was established in 1980 and has mostly been a compliance-driven organization, with "only modest discretionary funds available for reform and innovation," according to Arne Duncan, U.S. Secretary of Education.[6] The U.S. Department of Education is the federal agency that "establishes policy for, administers and coordinates most federal assistance to education." As it relates to SLDSs, the Department of Education collects data on America's schools and oversees research pertaining to the educational system. It oversees the execution of educational laws and policies enacted by Congress and the president, providing SEAs and LEAs with guidance and funding opportunities. "The Department's mission is to serve America's students— to promote student achievement and preparation for global competitiveness by fostering educational excellence and ensuring equal access."[7]

The National Center for Education Statistics (NCES) is the primary federal organization for "collecting and analyzing data related to education in the U.S. and other nations," according to its website. NCES is located within the U.S. Department of Education and the Institute of Education Sciences (IES). It funds grants for states and districts to set up and enhance their longitudinal data systems, almost $650 million since it started offering grants, at the time of publishing. NCES also developed the Common Educational Data Standard (CEDS) to aid educators in setting standards for the longitudinal data collected and shared.[8]

Regulatory History

From a regulation perspective, the first legislation to have impact on SLDSs came in 1994 with the federal School-to-Work Opportunities Act (STWOA). It stirred interest around tracking the transition from student to worker and work-readiness of American students. However, this legislation was not reauthorized after its initial five years.[9]

The next major law to impact the educational data landscape was the No Child Left Behind Act 2001 (NCLB). The core principle of NCLB is to raise student achievement, and thus it requires districts to track student data to show student, school, LEA, SEA and program progress. Since the law's implementation, school officials have begun to pay more attention to these data, using them to see changes in test scores over time and searching for potential ways to streamline district processes. In other words, NCLB pressed the issue and forced schools and all levels of educational agencies to take a hard look at their data and think of ways to improve their quality and quantity. However, one key weakness, as it pertains to data sharing and use, is that NCLB provides a one-way street in data sharing. The law requires data be reported to the government, but does not provide for those data to be supplied back to districts and teachers for use in education. The data NCLB requires to be reported are solely for reporting and judging purposes.[10]

In 2007, the America COMPETES Act codified the 12 elements that now define a P20 longitudinal data system. Based on the Data Quality Campaign's research and recommendations, to guide states in their independent establishment of an SLDS, the following data must be tracked and available for query under COMPETES:

1. A unique identifier for every student that does not permit a student to be individually identified (except as permitted by federal and state law)
2. The school enrollment history, demographic characteristics, and program participation record of every student
3. Information on when a student enrolls, transfers, drops out, or graduates from a school
4. Students' scores on tests required by the Elementary and Secondary Education Act
5. Information on students who are not tested, by grade and subject
6. Students' scores on tests measuring whether they're ready for college
7. A way to identify teachers and to match teachers to their students
8. Information from students' transcripts, specifically courses taken and grades earned
9. Data on students' success in college, including whether they enrolled in remedial courses
10. Data on whether K–12 students are prepared to succeed in college
11. A system of auditing data for quality, validity, and reliability
12. The ability to share data from preschool through postsecondary education data systems[11]

The America COMPETES Act Reauthorization of 2010 was signed by President Obama.

The American Recovery and Reinvestment Act of 2009 (ARRA, also known as the Stimulus Bill) reaffirmed the importance of the 12 elements set forth in the COMPETES Act. It required states, as a condition of receiving State Fiscal Stabilization Funds (SFSF), to commit to building a data system that consists of these elements. ARRA also established the Race to the Top (RTTT) program, making $4.35 billion available to states willing to lead the way in innovative approaches to prepare America's students for success.

The competitive RTTT program encouraged four core reforms, as Secretary Duncan noted in his July 2009 *Washington Post* article:

1. To reverse the pervasive dumbing-down of academic standards and assessments by states, Race to the Top winners need to work toward adopting common, internationally benchmarked K–12 standards that prepare students for success in college and careers.
2. To close the data gap—which now handcuffs districts from tracking growth in student learning and improving classroom instruction—states will need to monitor advances in student achievement and identify effective instructional practices.
3. To boost the quality of teachers and principals, especially in high-poverty schools and hard-to-staff subjects, states and districts should be able to identify effective teachers and principals—and have strategies for rewarding and retaining more top-notch teachers and improving or replacing ones who aren't up to the job.
4. Finally, to turn around the lowest-performing schools, states and districts must be ready to institute far-reaching reforms, from replacing staff and leadership to changing the school culture.[12]

To be eligible for RTTT funds, states must be approved for SFSF. To receive SFSF money, states must agree "to establish longitudinal data systems that include the elements set out in the America COMPETES Act."[13] Every single state signed off on this condition.[14]

In its first two phases, 11 states and the District of Columbia earned grant money: Delaware, District of Columbia, Florida, Georgia, Hawaii, Maryland, Massachusetts, New York, North Carolina, Ohio, Rhode Island, and Tennessee. (Florida and North Carolina will be highlighted in the case studies included in this book.) With another round of winners in 2011, 21 states and DC are now among the winners of RTTT funds.[15]

The Educational Technical Assistance Act of 2002 created the Institute of Education Sciences, which has administered competitive, cooperative agreement grants for SLDS. In November 2005, in conjunction with NCES, the SLDSS's Grant Program gave three-year grants to 14 states to aid in the designing, implementation or improvement of their SLDSs.[16] Twelve additional states and the District of Columbia were awarded grants in June 2007. In March 2009, 27 states received grants to enhance or establish SLDSs, including 15 new states. In May 2012, 24 states were given grants, with 8 new states making the cut.[17]

The guiding principle behind the NCES SLDS Grant Program—"Better decisions require better information"[18]—is also the motivation behind the whole SLDS movement. Despite many obstacles, states and educational systems continue to strive for more efficient, smarter data systems, with the financial support of the U.S. government and its agencies.

THE STATE OF SLDSs TODAY

Today, SDLSs are under way in most states, but their impact is yet to be fully realized. Every state has made some steps toward unifying its data, which is an indication of the growing national interest in using the data. The DQC's annual survey of states found consistent progress in growth in their 10 essential elements for SLDSs.[19] There are many challenges these systems face, as we discuss in this chapter, but it's worthwhile to consider how the system evolved into its current form.

For education, computers were used early on to store and maintain transcripts, and as time went on, gradebooks. In the 1970s, schools began including attendance and disciplinary data for each student, to allow for central reporting and sharing data between institutions. All these systems were generally independent, transactional systems that were designed to perform a single function. Technology that exists today to match student records across systems was not part of the mix; if there were two students in two different systems with the same name, it had to be manually resolved. Throughout the years, other single-purpose systems were added. Systems that met the required reporting needs by tracking free and reduced lunch spending and ones that track the bus routes each fulfilled a need within the state's data system and over time led to a complex, STLT data infrastructure. Each was operated independently by one department within the school system and shared data as requested. These siloed data systems were not interoperable, and though we use the past tense, many schools still operate in this way.

Current systems are more sophisticated, though interoperability with neighboring systems is still an issue. For instance, if a child moves from a school in Virginia to a new school in North Carolina, is there a seamless record transition from the old school to the new one, with no data lost? Even a move from one school district to another can result in information loss. If this child has a record in the social services system, will those records transfer as well? The technology and capabilities exist today to make this scenario seamless, though few states can do this. While we have made many advances since the transactional systems of 50 years ago, interoperability issues continue to plague our student records.

There has certainly been progress in recent years toward implementing and improving state systems, but there are still very discernible areas in which states are lagging. States generally do well regarding Governance structures, a data repository system, reporting and a research agenda, according to the DQC.[20] Linking data between agencies, providing access to stakeholders and teaching teachers how to use data appropriately are the key areas where little progress has been shown (and much is desired).[21] The DQC's key priorities for expanding and improving longitudinal data in states center around meeting the needs of the people in the state, with the greatest need for attention belonging to:

- Developing governance structures with authority
- Providing access to stakeholders (such as parents)
- Providing training to build stakeholders' capacity to use data to drive their educational decisions[22]

While there are many positive and encouraging gains being made in the field, the DQC cautions "the hardest work remains."[23] There are many cultural and systematic changes that require strong leadership and political will.

NCES SLDS grants have been integral in beginning the work it takes to get these systems going. Over the past 10 years, NCES has funded basic SLDS growth and development initiatives, designed to get K–12 systems up and functional. In the years to come, Commissioner Jack Buckley predicts, that funding will be drying up and NCES grants will focus more on developing data-use skills and capacity as well as expansion of systems to include early childhood data and workforce data.[24] The shift in funding priorities mirrors the DQC's analysis on the work that needs to be done to move SLDSs to the next level nationwide.

Challenges to SLDS Success

There are clear advantages to having an SLDS, and clear strategic reasons why they're important to the state and educational stakeholders. However, even when fully funded, they are difficult projects to institute. The barriers to SLDS initiatives are diverse, and as shown in Figure 2.1, largely relate to political and technological issues.

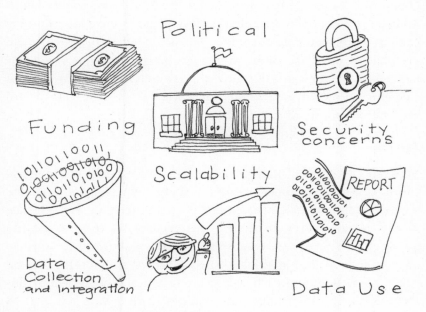

Figure 2.1 Challenges to SLDS Success

Funding

Thanks to the growing political will to create a more data-driven educational system, more and more government and independent grant funding is available, though winning this money has become more competitive. Creating and implementing an SLDS and its infrastructure is a potentially expensive undertaking, and winning grant money inevitably leads states to wonder what will become of the system they're building when the funding period ends. One way to overcome this barrier is to keep SLDS initiatives high on policy makers' radar, so that in spite of shifts in power and political pressures, the importance of educational data initiatives is understood universally. Proper planning and establishment of an engaged and active Governance structure are also important steps toward enabling continuity in SLDS projects, as discussed in Chapter 3.

Political

One of the biggest challenges to SLDS initiatives is not technical at all. While these kinds of projects are not new to many industries, educational agencies are fairly new to the game. And in the world of education, these data may be political. Several states have laws limiting or prohibiting matching of student data across different systems, and even federal laws place some restrictions on the exchange of individual records. In the cases of states with laws limiting data exchanges, changing or overturning arcane laws will be the first step toward meaningful data sharing.

Security

Between the laws in place to protect student privacy and political concerns among stakeholder groups about ownership of data, the security of the data to be shared and pooled is likely to pose a hurdle to any budding SLDS. To address this need, states can use security architectures already used extensively for large-scale, security-sensitive data projects within multinational companies and for the federal government. Solutions such as a secure technical processing environment that meets the Family Educational Record Privacy Act of 1974 (FERPA) and the Health Insurance Portability and Accountability Act

(HIPAA) restrictions for data privacy and role-based access for stake-holders and researchers enable states to address the security concerns of their stakeholding agencies as well as laws that apply to their data.

Data Collection and Integration Challenges

Traditionally, state departments of education have made investments in student information systems, finance systems and human resource management systems that aren't compatible, consolidated or easily integrated with one another. Further, according to the DQC, very few states can link their education data systems with other critical data systems that serve the same population, such as foster care, health, labor, juvenile justice and human services. In fact, it seems that in some cases, there is a significant interest in "fencing off" relevant data from the other agencies. A huge challenge lies in finding ways to con-solidate data in these related systems, and deciding which systems can be utilized in the establishment of an interoperable and unified SLDS. A true preschool-through-higher-education-and-workforce SLDS will require integration of data from many different agencies.

Scalability

Current processes and data systems often can't accommodate multiple school districts, let alone the entire state. What's certain is that the scope of data within an SLDS will only grow over time, so it's impor-tant that states invest in technology that can grow with the increase in data that is sure to come. The technology chosen for the SLDS also must have the flexibility to accommodate future technologies and business processes not yet defined. A gradual solution, providing for increased capability over time, is often the best answer to this issue since budgetary restrictions are almost always in play.

Creating a Culture of Data

For the ultimate purpose of an SLDS to be realized, the culture must undergo a change from seeing data as something the government requires for reporting and compliance purposes to something that is essential to evaluating the educational system's functioning and the primary tool to use for decision making. Simply setting up and implementing an SLDS doesn't provide for its integration into the day-to-day functions of the school system. Stakeholders, policy makers' SEAs and LEAs all have a role in ensuring the SLDS's use and utility.[25]

DATA MANAGEMENT MODELS

Each state will handle these decisions and policies differently, though two methods of organizing data and distributing responsibility have emerged as the most popular among the trailblazing states that are leading the way in implementing SLDSs and the states that have been the winners of federal grant money: the *federated data system* and *centralized data warehouse system*. Each is presented in this chapter, with greater detail provided in Chapter 4.

Both of the systems described require the establishment of a *student unique identifier* (UID) to facilitate interoperability standards of data furnished by multiple sources. The establishment of data quality practices and data governance policies should be in place to ensure the security of student data, quality of data being contributed to the SLDS, and common understanding of the SLDS's purpose and rules.

While each data design will organize the data and processes for querying in distinct ways (per their established requirements), all SLDSs can be expected to have certain capabilities and features. An SLDS will have a user interface that allows for querying and reporting, using student-level data displayed at an aggregate level with small cells suppressed. Additionally, it should have role-based accesses to allow different users to access different types of information. Teachers, parents, administrators and students all might have access, with different information available to them to suit their different roles in using the SLDS. For instance, a parent would be able to view school report cards through the education portal, to gauge the success of a certain district. LEA and SEA administrators could access the portal and run preformatted reports to comply with federal requirements. In any properly structured SLDS, confidentiality will be paramount and all legal requirements will be met or exceeded by means of confidentiality and privacy protections built into the system.

Centralized Data Warehouse

The centralized data warehouse model is the most widely applied method of organizing an SLDS. In this method, each agency supplies updated data daily (or with agreed-upon frequency) to a central database that houses all data collected. From the centralized data warehouse, reports and queries can be run internally using the data provided from each sector. Agencies are still responsible for their own data and retain their own databases. Using a combination of cloud-based and web-interfaced software, states are able to make this approach instantaneous, manageable and easy to use for constituents.

In a centralized data warehouse system, information is provided by the sectors that collect source data, spanning the P–12 and higher-education spectrum, as well as workforce agencies. These "data marts" are compiled using source system queries, and the data are pushed to the centralized data warehouse. All of the data are then combined and merged on the student UID record within the centralized data warehouse. Conversion of format to insure integration of the data from all constituent organizations can be done within the warehouse. However, standards that are established and enforced by the Governance body will eliminate the need for format conversion. The student data can be further enriched by linking to other local and state agency data, including juvenile justice, social services, and so on.

Michigan and Florida use this approach in their SLDS administration and have had tremendous success with it. Their case studies are included in this book.

Federated System

In the federated data system, each contributor to the SLDS (i.e., state-level Department of Public Instruction, universities, Employment Security Commission or comparable) represents a spoke with a central data broker in the center as the hub. A federated data system enables a requestor to send a query via the data broker hub that will transparently integrate multiple autonomous database systems into a single federated database, creating a result that includes updated data from multiple sources. The constituent databases are connected on a secure computer network and may be geographically decentralized. Once again, standards established by the Governance body are critical in the interoperability of agency source data, based on roles assigned by the Governance body.

For example, when a researcher, administrator or teacher has a question, he will query the database. The data broker will determine which agencies hold the data necessary to answer the questions and retrieve these data in report or dashboard display, joining duplicate records based on student UID as the key field. Extensive logging and other data safeguards are built into the system to assure data privacy and confidentiality of small cells and other classes of protected data.

Some states that employ this method, such as Wisconsin and North Carolina, find that a federated data system is a more effective approach. In this method, each agency is responsible for contributing its data to the system and maintaining its data to quality standards determined by the group. The data broker provides a fully integrated, logical composite of all constituent databases for reporting and research questions. This model allows for each party supplying data to the SLDS to have access to all of the others, without losing ownership of and responsibility for its own data. Systems that agencies have developed over years can still continue to be utilized in conjunction with this SLDS method. As with the centralized data warehouse, confidentiality laws and other legal concerns regarding student records are not affected.

CONCLUSION

The ability to ask questions across several systems and receive an on-demand answer is an invaluable asset to state and federal legislators, educators and researchers, with scores of potential benefits for our country's educational system. As America's standing among other countries' education systems continues to decline, it is essential that we have the data necessary to inform timely decision making to increase the quality of education for our country's youth. While implementing and improving these systems certainly poses many challenges, with strong leadership they can be overcome to benefit the nation's educational system.

NOTES

1. Data Quality Campaign, "National Data Summit: Welcome and Overview," January 2012, Aimee Rogstad Guidera, http://dataqualitycampaign.org/events/details/299 (accessed January 30, 2012).

2. Data Quality Campaign, Webcast (via SAS), Elizabeth Laird.

3. Jack Buckley, NCES MIS Conference Keynote, Washington, DC (February 13, 2013).

4. Data Quality Campaign, Webcast (via SAS), Elizabeth Laird.

5. Ibid.

6. Arne Duncan, "Education Reform's Moon Shot," *Washington Post* (July 24, 2009).

7. U.S. Department of Education, "What We Do," February 2, 2010, http://www2.ed.gov/about/what-we-do.html (accessed March 7, 2012).

8. NCES, "About Us," 2012, http://nces.ed.gov/about/ (accessed March 7, 2012).

9. Frank F. Furstenberg Jr. and David Neumark, "School-to-Career and Post-Secondary Education: Evidence from the Philadelphia Educational Longitudinal Study," IZA (Institute for the Study of Labor) (2005): 26.

10. Michelle R. Davis, "Finding Your Way in a Data-Driven World," *Education Week Digital Directions* (January 22, 2008): 5.

11. America COMPETES Act, Public Law 110–69, August 9, 2007, http://frwebgate.access.gpo.gov/cgi-bin/getdoc.cgi?dbname=110_cong_public_laws&docid=f:publ069.110.pdf.

12. Duncan, "Education Reform's Moon Shot."

13. NCES, Statewide Longitudinal Data Systems Grant Program, "Frequently Asked Questions," http://nces.ed.gov/programs/slds/faq_grant_program.asp#arra (accessed August 3, 2012).

14. Data Quality Campaign, "Data Quality Campaign," December 2011, http://dataqualitycampaign.org/files/DFA2011%20Mini%20report%20findings%20Dec1.pdf (accessed January 6, 2012).

15. U.S. Department of Education, "Department of Education Awards $200 Million to Seven States to Advance K–12 Reform," December 23, 2011, http://www.ed.gov/news/press-releases/department-education-awards-200-million-seven-states-advance-k-12-reform (accessed March 14, 2012).

16. Georges Vernez, Cathy Krop, Mirka Vuollo, and Janet S. Hansen, *Toward a K–20 Student Unit Record Data System for California* (Santa Monica, CA: Rand Corporation, 2008).

17. NCES, "About the SLDS Grant Program," 2011, http://nces.ed.gov/programs/slds/ (accessed March 7, 2012).

18. Ibid.

19. "Data for Action: Focus on People to Change Data Culture," Data Quality Campaign, November 2012, annual report.

20. Ibid.

21. Ibid.

22. Ibid.

23. Ibid.

24. Buckley, NCES MIS Conference Keynote.

25. Georgia Mariani, "Longitudinal Data Systems in Education," SAS, http://www.sas.com/resources/whitepaper/wp_9012.pdf (accessed in 2009).

CHAPTER **3**

Getting Started
on Your SLDS

An SLDS (statewide longitudinal data system) presents so many exciting and appealing possibilities in enabling better educational decisions, it's often hard to know where to start in getting the system off the ground. If you are in a state that is just getting started, or doing major renovations to your SLDS, this list can help to ensure you're addressing the key concerns to set up your system for future growth, use and success.

In this chapter, we discuss the key steps in preparing for your SLDS, as shown in Figure 3.1.

1. Establish a Data Governance Board.

2. Address *interoperability* of the data, ensuring all agencies use the same data definitions and compatible systems.

3. Set policies for *data security* and *student privacy* to ensure the SLDS is safer than current ad hoc systems.

4. Evaluate current systems and make connections to ensure the longitudinal data are in context and accessible to those who need them.

5. Make it sustainable to ensure the SLDS can thrive in life after grants.

Figure 3.1 Steps for SLDS Planning

SLDS PLANNING AND PREPARATION

There are many ways the idea and movement for an SLDS can be started. Often, it is mandated by the state government or pushed to priority through the receipt of federal grant dollars. In the beginning, there will be some scrambling to get everyone on the same page, in acceptance of the mission and the task, and to figure out just how an SLDS is established. In these early days, a data governance body is a vital group to give the project focus, leadership and momentum and establish the processes that give SLDSs a strong foundation. This is the very first task in setting up a new SLDS for success.

ESTABLISH A DATA GOVERNANCE BOARD

The Data Governance Board, or Governance, will be the leaders in the effort to establish the SLDS and make sense of the mission, grant regulations and other myriad forces at play. With representation from each stakeholder agency, and varying areas of expertise, Governance will lead the SLDS efforts and put leadership, talent and effort into the SLDS project. Thus, establishing this group of interested, invested advocates willing to help get it going is an essential first step in the SLDS planning process, setting the tone for the whole project. Setting up Governance can be conceived as the first step toward the cultural shift to data-driven action. By collectively investing time into data governance and initializing the SLDS project, each stakeholder agency will clearly see the benefits of access to such data as well as the importance of the system's upkeep and maintenance.

Governance should involve parties from each stakeholder agency (that is, anyone who might contribute or have access to the longitudinal data contained in the system). This cross-agency, cross-functional organizational structure is designed to establish mutual authority and consensus. It is essential that it not be viewed solely as an information technology project meant to be spearheaded by technology staff. While they should most certainly be included in Governance as subject-matter experts, the majority of Governance will be administrators and interested, nontechnical parties. Within the committee, there should be a designated leader to drive the meetings and discussions, as well as subcommittees to take deeper dives into big issues as they arise. The team should meet often in the early stages to ensure the momentum is strong and the project is able to meet deadlines that might be associated with grant monies.

Bringing together all of the parties to an SLDS might be challenging at first, with each group having paved their own way in data governance in the past. Each agency will have some means of collecting and handling its data, but after years of figuring it out on their own, there will likely be vast differences between systems.[1] The inherent problems in the current method of tracking and sharing student data—lack of consistency, interoperability and access—are the very reasons Governance is challenging and crucial. Given these near-universal weaknesses, coupled with the millions of dollars being invested in the SLDS, getting Governance off to a good start is vital. There is much work to be done and a great deal at stake.

Why Governance Is Important

Governance will be a driving force behind the SLDS project at every step of the way. From the initial information gathering and asset inventory to the ongoing maintenance and improvement efforts, this group of stakeholders will work together to insure the security and future of this state asset. *Data governance* is defined by IES (Institute of Education Sciences) as "overall management of the availability, usability, integrity, quality, and security of data."[2] So, Governance's responsibility is to get the stakeholders for the SLDS on the same page regarding data that are to be shared, and establish policies and processes for the system to govern its use in the future. Setting the rules of the system prior to its establishment is highly preferable to troubleshooting issues that arise after the fact.[3]

Governance brings many benefits to all stakeholders. Getting this step right can set the SLDS up for long-term buy-in and success.[4] Governance will *establish ownership and authoritative sources of data*, which therein dictates responsibility and accountability on the quality of specific data to certain agencies. Through the processes of establishing ownership and data standards, Governance will *identify and resolve redundancies*. Governance will enable and push a *gradual move toward data standardization* insuring that different agencies' data are interoperable and accessible. One major outcome of Governance is a *shift from reactive to proactive* in how data are dealt with. As issues get resolved, Governance can move from addressing issues that exist to forecasting and prevention.

Through all of these exercises, reviews and discussions, for better or worse, a *better understanding of data assets* is inevitable. When Governance collaborates and makes decisions associated with standardization, a heightened awareness of the state's and agencies' data assets will occur. As stakeholders work and deal with the data, they will come to see them as an asset, better understanding what is available and how best to utilize the data to improve educational outcomes.

First Steps for Governance

After Governance is established, it's time to get started building the state's SLDS. The steps that follow, as articulated in the list at the beginning of the chapter, are important first tasks for the new committee to give attention to.

An SLDS contains historic data that can be combined with current data to affect future outcomes. In today's economic and educational climate, this is a vital technological stride. Each member of Governance should consider how a fully realized SLDS might change the equation for their organizations and for their students. Effective and inspirational Governance can establish a culture of innovation among educational entities, ensuring that all suggestions and objections are expressed and considered, encouraging collaboration and out-of-the-box thinking. In short, the whole is greater than the sum of its parts. For reluctant partners in this endeavor, consider emphasizing the benefits to be gained by each stakeholder group, in hopes of showing the importance of publishing and subscribing to the SLDS and compelling cooperation and collaboration. This will eclipse the institutional status-quo mentality to resist change. Showing the potential long-term benefits to each member of the group is key to eliciting cooperation early on.[5]

ADDRESS INTEROPERABILITY OF THE DATA

A major prerequisite for having an SLDS that can provide accurate answers is that the data accessed from different sources are compatible and share a common student UID (unique identifier). Governance should establish policies surrounding data standards and student UIDs statewide to ensure that the data going into the system are in the correct format and matched to the correct UID so that results are accurate.

Data Standards: CEDS

Having disparate technical systems and data definitions is passable for the compliance and reporting required in the current paradigm. Often, compliance reports occur within one agency but require multiple collections of the same data using different systems. Many states and local districts have developed their own data systems for longitudinal data that meet the goals they currently have, but, because of different standards and definitions, cannot be easily integrated or matched with other systems. For states to provide longitudinal data for educational decisions they're currently facing (and will continue to face) data standards must be negotiated and implemented to provide order, focus and efficiency. Governance will define a common standard to be followed by all parties to the SLDS, insuring an interoperable system.

When we use the term *data standard,* three different types of data standards are encompassed in this definition as it applies to an SLDS. One type of data standard involves the data definition and code set for a certain data element—a simple definition of what is represented in a certain data element. For instance, for the data element that holds a student's first name, the definition might be "the full legal first name given to a person at birth, baptism, or through legal change."[6] A second type of data standard involves the technical specifications or attribute, a definition that would be useful to those engineering the SLDS and providing technical criteria and requirements, as well as methods and processes for data. This could include limitations on data field length or makeup. In the example of the data element holding the student's first name, this could include a character limit, and instructions that the first character is to be capitalized. The final type of data standard encompasses guidelines and relationship information for each field. Showing how fields relate to one another within and among student and teacher records requires a standardized data model to provide the context.[7] In the example of the student's name, the data standard might include information relating it to the last and middle name, showing that the three fields in the prescribed order constitute the student's name.

Where should you start in getting the necessary educational agencies mapping to the same standard? The Common Education Data Standards (CEDS) was developed by the National Center for Education Statistics (NCES) and is now in its third version. CEDS is now a widely accepted and supported standard among educational agencies and LDS software products. This nearly universal "technical blueprint" for collecting and maintaining student data enables sharing across entities and product development.[8] CEDS essentially provides a common definition of the data to be collected by and used by stakeholding agencies so that states can turn their attention to data use. CEDS is so prevalent in the SLDS world that it is the only data standard to be discussed in this book.

This standard sets forth rules on which data fields are collected by local and state educational agencies. CEDS is a "specified set of the most commonly used education data elements to support the effective exchange of data within and across states, as students transition between educational sectors and levels, and for federal reporting."[9] Promoting a common vocabulary among and between educational systems allows for more consistent, more comparable data to exist at each agency.

CEDS was developed with input from stakeholders at all levels of the education system: the U.S. Department of Education, the Department of Health and Human Services, the Department of Labor, LEAs, SEAs, Institutes of Higher Education, as well as educational foundations and associations.[10] CEDS, then, is the result of a collaborative effort between the U.S. Department of Education and all levels of schools and educational agencies and various national organizations.

CEDS was designed to replace the vendor-driven standards landscape, which made it difficult for educational systems to be interoperable. The federal government will never officially mandate a standard, but in CEDS it essentially provides an alternative to vendor standards that takes the successful and useful pieces of what the vendor community has created and makes one comprehensive standard: CEDS.

CEDS is a *data dictionary* and a *data model*. A data dictionary provides definitions of data elements, including the name of the element (to ensure all parties are using the same terminology) and interpretation (to ensure everyone has the same understanding of what is included in each data field). A data dictionary also includes a description of what values are allowed (such as ranges and character limits) and other properties and constraints on each field. The data dictionary provides a robust and expanding common voluntary vocabulary. Looking at the data in an SLDS as an orchestra, CEDS tunes each instrument and gives each musician the sheets of music. Without CEDS (the conductor), the orchestra would be cacophonous, with no synchronicity to its melodies. With the CEDS data dictionary, the musicians can each play the same song and make beautiful music together.[11]

A data model is the documented logical definition of entities as groups of elements and inter-entity relationships. The CEDS Logical Data Model is comprised of two distinct views: the Domain Entity Schema and the Normalized Data Schema. Broadly, the data model shows how the data fields relate to one another, connections that will enable greater analysis and insight into the data down the road.

CEDS is a useful and comprehensive data standard; however, getting educational data mapped to CEDS isn't instantaneous. Once a state and its Governance have agreed upon CEDS as their universal standard, a timeline and process should be agreed to for each agency to ensure that their data are mapped correctly. After the agreement upon the standard, Governance must make sure the path is clear and that there aren't any major barriers to wide adoption of the standard.

Student Unique Identifiers

A crucial step to a state's ability to establish a truly interoperable SLDS is, broadly, its ability to match student records accurately across each institution contributing data. If two students in the same grade have the same name, how does the state prevent student data from being intermingled and confused? How does a state provide the means to retain anonymity when conveying student data to a party not privy to confidential student data? Many educational entities identify students now in rather complicated and conflicting ways. With differing systems across institutions, matching student records necessarily involves using several fields of personally identifying information (PII), which, taken together, identify an individual using a coded identifier and logical algorithms to avoid mismatches. For instance, a first name, last name, date of birth and address, associated with some logical code to create an identifier, might create a student unique identifier (UID) for a student in one district. While this system is manageable across institutions, there are security and data accuracy concerns to be raised when sharing data with outside parties. The simplest and most effective system for an SLDS to use to match student records, and the one recommended by the Department of Education, Data Quality Campaign and the authors of this book, is a statewide student UID.

A UID is a required element of a longitudinal data system under the America COMPETES Act, providing a means for students to be identified in an anonymous way by something other than their name or Social Security number. It is, then, the key first step in enabling student records to be matched across agencies and the interoperability of that data. Many K–12 institutions and SEAs have either begun or implemented systems to track UIDs for students.

SET POLICIES FOR DATA SECURITY AND STUDENT PRIVACY

The next task Governance will tackle will be how each agency should handle data security and privacy of confidential student information. Paramount to any data system is the issue of security and student information privacy. While many laws and policies have impacted the development and operation of SLDSs, when it comes to student information, the Family Educational Record Privacy Act of 1974 (FERPA) is the law with the biggest impact on SLDSs. It has been updated periodically to address changing technology and access. It explicitly names the student as the owner of his student record and SEAs, LEAs, and other educational entities as the second party to those records, responsible for maintaining them. It puts forth strict rules about what can be shared when individual identity can be ascertained, guarding against the release of student data to a third party. FERPA allows for sharing of student data from a second party to a third party, provided PII is obscured.[12] Under FERPA, deidentified data files may be shared without student or parent consent.

Among Department of Education–funded educational institutions and agencies, sharing student record data is authorized under FERPA. So, for SLDSs, sharing raw data among educational agencies is legal and encouraged. Additionally, FERPA authorizes educational entities to share student data with workforce or other noneducation agencies for certain, approved purposes: evaluating federal or state-supported education programs, or enforcing legal compliance with programs.[13] As the custodians of a student's educational data, there are many responsibilities education agencies must take on to stay within the law while sharing data among other educational agencies and with the public.

Privacy: Protecting Personally Identifying Information

Governance should see to it that the proper protections are in place to guarantee the privacy of individual student records. There are several instances that arise when reporting data to the public (as schools are obligated to do) where private student data might be easily traced back to the student and inadvertently disclose protected information. Information such as the student's name, parents' names, Social Security number or UID, even the student's date of birth are considered PII.

FERPA introduces the concept of what a *reasonable person* might be able to deduce as the standard by which educational agencies are obligated to suppress PII. In public reports, the smaller the dataset being shared, the more an educational agency has to watch for ways in which a reasonable person might be able to figure out undisclosed information. Small cell size doesn't automatically mean there will be disclosure, but without a doubt, it increases the risk of a disclosure.[14] Instances emerge where student data might be obvious in a small cell; for instance, the only African American boy in the third grade at a certain school could easily be identified, even if he is not named.[15]

Even in larger cells there can be opportunities for identification. For instance, in a group of 100 African American third-grade students, if one fails the grade and the other 99 students pass, the family of the one who failed essentially knows the other 99 African American children passed if that statistic is shared publicly. There are many instances like this where revealing certain information can lead to a reasonable individual figuring out protected information. In cases like this where even after PII is restricted and there's a chance the student could be identified, agencies are obligated to use certain techniques to obscure the data to maintain the confidentiality of the individual. According to Michael Hawes, Statistical Privacy Advisor to the U.S. Department of Education, there are three recommended methods that the NCES endorses to protect personally identifiable information: *suppression*, *blurring* and *perturbation*.

Suppression entails leaving some data out to protect the identity of small subsets of data. It can be accomplished through removing data to prevent the identification of individuals in small cells or with unique characteristics. Another way to suppress data is to publish only a small sample instead of the entire dataset.[16] Blurring is a tactic that decreases the precision of data to avoid disclosing personal information. It introduces uncertainty to a dataset, protecting small cells. Blurring can be accomplished by aggregation with larger datasets; more individuals make it harder to find one individual. For instance, combining several races into one group rather than listing them individually could successfully blur data. Blurring could also be accomplished through the use of percentages (96 percent of 200 could be a few different raw numbers), ranges (between 5 and 10), top or bottom coding (greater than 95 percent), or rounding (all data rounded to nearest 5).[17] Perturbation involves making some changes to the data to reduce certainty. Some perturbation methods include: data swapping, introducing noise (adding 1 or subtracting 1 from certain categories) and using models based on trends to generate fake numbers that mirror the actual data without portraying it exactly.[18]

The 2011 amendments to FERPA put a lot of responsibility on LEAs and SEAs to come up with policies on what access is needed by whom. Many longitudinal software solutions will provide the means to execute these data privacy protection tactics.[19] In the establishment of Governance, policies will be established for how schools should handle public reporting to protect PII and increase transparency.

Data Security

Data security is distinctly different from individual protection, though data security impacts the educational agency's ability to provide individual protection. Data security refers to the agency's ability to prevent unauthorized access to private student information, and its ability to allow access to authorized parties. The sharing associated with an SLDS certainly puts a finer point on this capability of an agency's data system. Having the ability to share and shield certain student information is a responsibility states should take very seriously, as it has legal implications. In the process of setting up the SLDS, Governance will evaluate current systems' security and establish a system-wide protocol.

The first step in securing an educational agency's data is to perform an inventory and gain an accurate picture of the *information landscape* for each data system as it exists currently. To protect an agency's data, Governance must have a full picture of what data they hold. This is part of Governance's responsibilities, though their ability to thoroughly perform this task will depend on each agency's compliance and helpfulness. The evaluation process is described in detail in the next section.

Role-Based Access

The best way to control access to certain levels of student information is based on a user's credentials. A primary responsibility of Governance will be to outline the different user groups that will need or desire access to the longitudinal data and determine which levels of access each is entitled to.[20] The technical structure of this role-based system may differ depending on how a state constructs its SLDS; however, some level of role-based access is recommended for any SLDS. Governance should establish several user groups and outline their entitled level of access, using the information learned about the data each agency holds and the accompanying sensitivity of those fields.

Varying levels of access by roles requires a strong maintenance process and coordination across agencies. Sustainability is a concern, as individuals can hold multiple roles throughout their careers. For instance, a teacher can also be a parent. These issues will require ongoing attention and discussion by Governance.

EVALUATE CURRENT SYSTEMS AND MAKE CONNECTIONS

K–12 systems have existed for several years. Given this fact, interoperability will need to be addressed early on, as all systems are unlikely to be in compatible formats. Even if a state is establishing its first K–12 longitudinal data system, it must have an eye toward how the system will grow to include data from other sources in the future. This inclusion of workforce, social services, health, higher education and early childhood data (to name a few) is the next frontier for SLDSs.

Link to Data Systems Outside of K–12

In a true preschool-through-school-college-and-workforce (P20W) SLDS, educators will have access to data about students before they enter Kindergarten as well as after they leave the K–12 data system. That is information not only on where they went to college and how they fared, but from after they entered the workforce. Data such as their first job, first salary and career field could be connected with their high school transcript to help schools make inferences about what factors enable students to achieve career success. As more states establish and refine their K–12 systems, extending to other data sources is the next step.[21] In the early stages, figuring out which agencies are providing the needed data and how those systems will connect is essential.

Connecting data with agencies outside the K–12 system poses many challenges in interoperability and logistics. Though these connections with preschool and postgraduate and workforce agencies are an important part of the SLDS picture, and the true essence of a P20W system, they pose many challenges and necessitate strong working relationships among agencies.

Connecting student data in this way will require working with stakeholding agencies that likely have data to contribute but not much to gain from it, posing unique challenges in bridging the gap between education and workforce agencies in the establishment of an SLDS.

There aren't many recommended standards for compliance with agency stakeholders who are outside the educational arena.

Take, for example, the process of connecting student records with their workforce records. This connection most often requires the state department of labor (or department of employment) to participate, matching records and furnishing data back to the SLDS. The data, once obtained, are invaluable to states in judging how well their students' courses of study prepared them to enter a given field—which were most successful and, perhaps, which couldn't find jobs easily or at all. So, how does a state accomplish this linkage successfully, both on a political and a policy level? The link between educational data and workforce data is tricky. The Wage Record Interchange System (WRIS) was established for all 50 states to share unemployment data and wage records in the aggregate format for Department of Labor (DOL) projects. WRIS2 is a newer agreement, with only 25 states signed on currently, which gives states the ability to create data-sharing agreements beyond those needed for DOL purposes. This agreement allows more leeway and might facilitate SLDS sharing among participating states' DOL and SLDSs, though there is still a lot of red tape (in the form of memoranda of understanding needed and FERPA compliance).[22] Workforce uses Social Security numbers to identify individuals while educational systems are encouraged to use UIDs. Often, a bridge can be built to match the records (sometimes using an outside agency, such as the Department of Motor Vehicles [DMV]) with a great degree of validity. There are more avenues to connecting to workforce data than ever before, and hopefully in the years to come, even more connections will be made.

While there is no set standard for achieving high levels of buy-in from non-educational agencies, there are several best practices noted among states that have set up a productive, mutual working relationship between partner agencies and their SLDS.

Reinforce Mutual Benefit from Linkage

Indiana's SLDS committee noted the importance of remembering that establishing linked systems for the educational data system is first and foremost a research project, not simply a technology project.[23] This statement underscores the trap it's easy to fall into when committees are in the thick of SLDS planning and implementation—that it's all about the technology. While there are substantial concerns relating to technology, keeping focused on the motivation behind the implementation and data sharing is crucial to the success of incorporating workforce agencies into the group.

Continually reinforcing the benefit to all throughout the implementation and enhancement of an SLDS is an ongoing task for stakeholders. Keeping the added value front and center is ideal for maintaining a positive working relationship.

There is often a protective mind-set about data among groups with data to share—sharing data is not something agencies are historically eager to do.[24] The agency's fears might stem from a fear that others will use the data to embarrass the agency (either intentionally or not), or that the data will be misinterpreted or misrepresented. The sharing conversation quickly circles back to data standards, as the proper interpretation of data elements can avert the feared misinterpretation and inadvertent misrepresentation by outside parties.[25]

Overcoming this resistance to reshaping the culture of state agencies to one of mutual benefit, trust and data sharing is a challenge, indeed. Continually reinforcing the "something in it for everyone" benefit of sharing data—school and student outcome improvement certainly benefits everyone—is a recommended tactic.

Common Data Dictionary

The question of interoperability is once again a primary issue to emerge when two different data systems attempt to share data. However, if the educational community of a state is mapped to CEDS, this will help in the ease of establishing a data dictionary as it applies to a particular outside stakeholding agency. Since it is not feasible to expect an organization such as the Department of Labor to adopt CEDS universally (it doesn't apply to them, by and large), it is more feasible to establish a separate and more targeted data dictionary for data exchange with workforce agencies, including only the data that will need to be shared. CEDS 3.0 is set to include additional standards for post-secondary, early childhood and workforce data that will aid in navigating this space immensely.[26]

Memoranda of Understanding

A common method for insuring that all parties to a project are on the same page regarding expectations is to circulate and obtain a signed memorandum of understanding (MOU) from all parties. This documentation provides information for each agency to refer back to, and can inform their conduct and policies as well as give them confidence that the other parties to the agreement are to be trusted.

Privacy and Security of Data

These MOUs will no doubt contain information establishing the processes surrounding data encryption, destruction of data, access to data and what sort of purposes data may or may not be used for. The policies established by Governance (as discussed in Chapter 2) should be reflected in MOUs. Indeed, as a best practice, workforce agencies will be represented in Governance and will have their voice heard in the establishment of these policies.

Record Matching

"The real key to interoperability is the matching of records."[27] Indeed, what good is obtaining workforce information if the data systems cannot distinguish between two persons with the same name? Developing a matching system that accurately makes matches based on identifiers used by each agency is a crucial step for states in establishing these data channels. Several states share data with their state workforce agency, which generally uses Social Security numbers as identifiers with a bridge to match SSNs to the student UID the educational data system uses. These *fuzzy-match* systems use several algorithms that look at multiple variables to confirm likely matches, and can be highly accurate, preserving the protection of confidential student data but allowing for records to be matched.[28]

Voluntary Partnerships

In establishing working relationships with partner agencies, it is essential to keep in mind the voluntary nature of these partnerships. Often, the impetus behind the establishment of a P20W SLDS is a grant award and encouragement from state officials, not a law mandating its establishment and each agency's compliance. Indeed, the operation of an SLDS is not a dictatorship but a democracy, with each party contributing and using information coming to the table having the right to be heard and have their needs met. This, of course, applies and is particularly important for peripherally related partner agencies to the SLDS with crucial information to contribute. It is, as always, important to work together to achieve the goal of establishing a data link rather than command a workforce agency to share its data.

Inventory of Current Systems

Given the current state of student data and SLDSs, the need for improvement is documented and widely acknowledged. To improve, educational agencies of all levels must be open to restructuring some of the systems they have established and utilized in the past. However, a workable, affordable and reasonable SLDS should allow states to continue using data that's been collected and, potentially, keep some systems that they've spent years establishing and utilizing. Indeed, a criterion upon which states should evaluate the appropriateness of an SLDS solution should be its ability to augment the work that has been done on student data collection and maintenance. Where prudent, incorporating existing structures and processes should be viewed as a way to make the SLDS implementation easier.

As part of Governance's information-gathering process and evaluation of data security, a data and system inventory will be executed. A clear understanding of what they are working with will inevitably impact how the resulting system is configured. In other words, if an SLDS is where the state is going, where are they *now*? This information can be learned through surveys, interviews, or group meetings, and there are many variations on the assessment that states might customize to fit their unique circumstances. While it should involve interviews with IT personnel, the most valuable feedback on the assessment will most likely come from the users and administrators of the system.[29]

States should survey each agency to learn what data elements are collected and stored, and what the process is for handling these records.

Governance should make sure to gain a clear understanding of each agency's data quality procedures and risks. To engineer a solution that addresses each agency's needs, it is critical that a clear understanding be achieved for what purposes the data are accessed. It is important to understand where the agency stands in readiness to collaborate on the SLDS project.[30]

MAKE IT SUSTAINABLE

SLDSs take years to establish, with a substantial time commitment involved in the planning and implementation phases. Additionally, SLDSs are only an asset when multiple years of data exist. These realities mean that even in the best scenarios, it will take years before a state's SLDS can embody all of the benefits on which it's sold. They are, unarguably, a long-term investment that makes it even more necessary to keep them up and running for a long time and continually communicate with stakeholders to prove their worth. Often, high levels of federal funding are at stake and the need to get the system right is strong. There are a few key areas to consider when addressing the sustainability of your SLDS.

Solutions That Can Grow with the System

The amount of data your SLDS tracks will only grow in the foreseeable future. Though there should be discussions and procedures for archiving old data, the key student longitudinal data will be on record for years to come and will increase quickly, as more students enter and leave the school system. Considering this fact, it is important for the SLDS process to include sustainability and long-term growth projections in its decision regarding software and hardware solutions. Once parts of the SLDS are up and running, usage will grow and users will continue to ask more sophisticated questions, and thus the reporting and analysis will continue to become more complex. SLDS projects often aim to include non-K–12 datasets as well (such as early childhood and workforce data), so ensuring that the system can incorporate these data is also important. This growth also underscores the importance of establishing best practices early in the project for data governance, security and standards, as issues will only compound as the amount of data being maintained increases.

Budget

If a state has won government grant money to set up a functional SLDS, it understands it is receiving a set amount of funding over a finite period. The funding will end; this is a fact of life for SLDS development, implementation and functioning. Therefore, it is imperative that grant funds are not the only fuel keeping an SLDS project running. Having a strategic plan for what happens once the federal or independent grant money is no longer available is necessary. Continually looking to the future, budgeting and planning is the best way to safeguard the system's future.

With the caveat that each state's situation will be different, it can cost $1 million per year per stakeholder agency for the first three years of SLDS planning and implementation. Factors such as the condition of existing data systems, the size of the state and its dataset, and the chosen software solutions will affect this number; it is important to acknowledge that the cost of this system can be high and to set the expectation accordingly. Seeking funds from the state legislature, independent grant monies or additional federal funds are good options for obtaining a greater investment to kick-start SLDS activities. Showing the ways in which an SLDS will make other line items in the educational budget more streamlined is a good strategy to work toward overcoming budgetary shortfalls and objections. The commitment from the government must be able to rise above changes in political leadership and agenda.

Maintain Support—Communicate

A key factor at every crossroad in the development, implementation and improvement of an SLDS is enthusiasm and buy-in among users and leaders within the state's educational community. There is clear value to having longitudinal data, new and innovative ways to use data that can revolutionize the way education is administered and process improvements that can save all agencies time and resources.

However, establishing an ideal SLDS is a process and sustaining high levels of support, even in transitional phases where demands on resources might be high, is one of the biggest battles a state may face. Communication with stakeholders is vital to maintaining support.

In the beginning, selling stakeholders on the benefits of an SLDS—the things it can do to change their day-to-day job responsibilities and change the system for the better—is very important. If your state is lucky enough to win federal grant money to start or augment an SLDS, share the news, and continue to update the community as the project progresses. This is a system with very real and tangible benefits for stakeholders, and improvements that the general population can easily get behind. For the general public, a great interest exists in updating and making more efficient our educational data systems and management of schools. At each step of the way in garnering and maintaining high levels of support among stakeholders and the public, it is vital to efficiently and honestly communicate progress and intention with your audiences.

State Support

If feasible, establishing legislative support for the SLDS is a best practice. Either through funding for the system or by passing legislation that codifies the major tenets of the SLDS into law and mandating compliance, lawmakers can provide the reinforcement to ensure the state's support of the SLDS.[31] As a state applies for an SLDS grant from the federal government, it is a good idea to enlist the support of the state government in this effort. Ideally, this means getting in your state's budget to augment federal funds. Advocating for increased (and ongoing) investment in the SLDS can set up the system for high levels of buy-in early on, as well as a better level of sustainability as time goes on. Another key concern, where state politics are concerned, is positioning this issue as a non-partisan, universal issue so that a change in leadership does not derail your SLDS project. Education is in a precarious position politically in many states, and often falls prey to budget cuts. Establish wide and strong political support at the state level to safeguard your SLDS.

Leadership within Agencies

When Governance is established, it is quite likely that there will be several "champions" of the SLDS, folks who are excited about making it happen, who clearly see the collective benefit and are willing and able to be ambassadors for the project. These champions are invaluable and should be identified early and cultivated.

Through the initial phases of an SLDS project, maintaining buy-in from all of the agencies contributing to the system is sure to have some glitches and missteps. Having champions within each stakeholding agency can aid in smoothing rough spots and diplomatic handling of sensitive issues among peers. As support and enthusiasm might falter for the SLDS, the champions can help to bring interest back and keep stakeholders focused on the goal. Recognizing these ambassadors early in the process is a best practice.

Make the System Invaluable

The shift to a culture of data that we discuss in this book is the final way we suggest making your SLDS invaluable to its users. Perhaps now, in your state's current paradigm, longitudinal data are peripheral and superfluous. In the years to come as the system gets implemented and begins producing timely and actionable data, these data will drive decisions and change the way things are done within schools. Once that shift has occurred and stakeholders clearly see the benefit, the thought of removing that asset from the mix is inconceivable. Though this sort of value alone cannot be a sustainer for the system, showing the value it adds and the impact it has had on educators and school administration can create a level of grassroots support that will make sustaining the system easier.

CONCLUSION

Establishing an SLDS is a tall order, but proper planning is an integral first step to the eventual success of the project. It is designed to be a permanent, game-changing solution to educational data issues that have persisted for years, and should be approached with requisite deliberation and dedication. The most essential of the steps we give in this chapter is Governance, as it sets the tone for the entire project. Governance is not about control but rather leadership, and a good Governance will keep the momentum and support for the SLDS high throughout the project. Setting standards early on for data, policies on sharing and security are also vital building blocks upon which your system will reside.

NOTES

1. National Forum on Educational Statistics, *Traveling Through Time: The Forum Guide to Longitudinal Data Systems, Book 1 of 4: What Is an LDS?* (Alexandria, VA: ED Publications, 2010), http://nces.ed.gov/pubsearch/pubsinfo.asp?pubid=2010805.

2. IES, Statewide Longitudinal Data System Grant Program, "P-20W Data Governance: Tips from States," May 2012, http://nces.ed.gov/programs/slds/pdf/brief4_P_20W_DG.pdf (accessed August 13, 2012).

3. National Forum on Educational Statistics, *Traveling Through Time, Book 1 of 4.*

4. Ibid., *Book 3 of 4.*

5. Georges Vernez, Cathy Krop, Mirka Vuollo, and Janet S. Hansen, *Toward a K–20 Student Unit Record Data System for California* (Santa Monica, CA: Rand Corporation, 2008).

6. CEDS, "CEDS Elements, Version 4," 2011, http://ceds.ed.gov/elements.aspx (accessed March 14, 2012).

7. National Forum on Educational Statistics, *Traveling Through Time.*

8. DQC Webinar, "How the New Common Education Data Standards Can Support Policy and Practice," http://dataqualitycampaign.org/events/details/301?utm_source=Data+Quality+Campaign&utm_campaign=0830f0c28e-2_23_CEDS_V2_webinar_survey2_23_2012&utm_medium=email (accessed February 23, 2012).

9. NCES, "Common Education Data Standards," 2012, http://nces.ed.gov/programs/ceds/ (accessed March 12, 2012).

10. CEDS, "What Is CEDS?," 2012, http://ceds.ed.gov/whatIsCEDS.aspx (accessed March 15, 2012).

11. MIS Conference, "Mapping to CEDS," presentation (February 15, 2012).

12. Family Educational Rights and Privacy Act (FERPA), http://www.ed.gov/policy/gen/guid/fpco/ferpa/index.html. 20 U.S.C. § 1232g; 34 CFR Part 99.

13. Education Counsel, LLC, "U.S. Department of Education Final FERPA Regulations: Advisory and Overview," December 2, 2011, http://www.dataqualitycampaign.org/files/2011%20Final%20FERPA%20Regulations_Advisory%20and%20Overview%20FINAL.pdf (accessed October 11, 2012).

14. Michael Hawes, "Protection of Personally Identifiable Information through Disclosure Avoidance Techniques," NCES Conference (February 15, 2012).

15. National Forum on Educational Statistics, *Traveling Through Time.*

16. Hawes, "Protection of Personally Identifiable Information through Disclosure Avoidance Techniques."

17. Ibid.

18. National Forum on Educational Statistics, *Traveling Through Time*.

19. Hawes, "Protection of Personally Identifiable Information through Disclosure Avoidance Techniques."

20. National Forum on Educational Statistics, *Traveling Through Time*.

21. Jack Buckley, NCES MIS Conference Keynote, Washington, DC (February 13, 2013).

22. Kate Louton and Baron Rodriguez, "Labor and Education Data Sharing 101," Management Information Systems (MIS) Conference, IES (February 13, 2013).

23. Data Quality Campaign, "Using Linked Data to Drive Education and Training Improvement," October 2010, http://dataqualitycampaign.org/resources/details/1050 (accessed April 10, 2012).

24. Ibid.

25. Vernez, Krop, Vuollo, and Hansen, *Toward a K–20 Student Unit Record Data System for California*.

26. Jack Buckley, "Common Education Data Standards," June 2012, National Center for Education Statistics, http://www.slideshare.net/edpublishers/common-education-data-standards-jack-buckley (accessed October 16, 2012).

27. Data Quality Campaign, "Using Linked Data to Drive Education and Training Improvement."

28. Ibid.

29. National Forum on Educational Statistics, *Traveling Through Time*.

30. Ibid.

31. Ibid.

CHAPTER 4

Data Management: Creating One Version of the Truth

A crucial and challenging decision states face when combining multiple, disparate databases to constitute an SLDS (statewide longitudinal data system) is how the data will be managed. For instance, combining a database with elementary school student records and a database that holds middle school student records within the same school system, there will inevitably be commonalities in those records. That is, students who went from fifth to sixth grade will be listed in both repositories. Certainly, students will transfer schools within the state and be listed in both databases, and if a student goes to college and subsequently enters the workforce, he'll be listed in each database. Add overlaps that could occur with partner agencies, like a state workforce agency, and there are even more issues in data standards and management processes. How does the SLDS decide which students are the same? How does the SLDS decide which record has the most up-to-date information? Having a process for answering these questions that are sure to come up (and come up often) is essential for the functioning of an SLDS. Having quality, trustworthy and actionable data is vital to the survival of the SLDS. Keeping the data organized, accurate and in good quality are challenges that can be overcome with sound data management procedures.

This chapter will primarily discuss *master data management* (MDM) as a concept states can use to frame their data governance exercises and SLDS construction. MDM is broad and can provide many helpful strategies to states and Governance as they begin to map out the technical format of their SLDS. *Data quality*, *metadata management* and the *architecture* of the state's database system are also important MDM-based decisions to be carefully considered. It isn't something that states must do in their SLDS planning and execution efforts, but we recommend adopting this philosophy to guide the efforts of the Governance and provide context and continuity for their efforts, creating a more agile system equipped to handle change.

WHAT IS MASTER DATA MANAGEMENT?

To start this discussion, we will define master data management (MDM) as: synchronized, defined and uniformed business data processes that facilitate consistent, reliable data to feed every operational and decision-support application, giving stakeholders access to accurate data.

MDM is a way to intelligently consolidate and manage data and deliver a more unified view of the enterprise across applications and platforms. Though it is most often associated with large corporations and their databases and business processes, it has many valuable applications for SLDS management. MDM integrates information from existing data sources, consolidating these sources into a master reference file, which then feeds information back to the sources, creating accurate and consistent data across the enterprise. In an SLDS scenario, this is a game-changing way to manage data. After MDM practices are fully integrated into an SLDS system, a user could update a student record from one location and the changes would be visible instantaneously to all users of the system.

Master data refers to the nontransactional information that an organization tracks: the persons, places and things. In an SLDS, an example of master data is most of the student identifying information (name, address, gender and so on). MDM is the process of creating one common, correct data record for each student.

MDM is widely accepted among large corporations. Many businesses find that when managed well, high-quality data can propel their business forward, making mergers and acquisitions more streamlined and making regulatory compliance simpler. It can provide that elusive *single view* of customers or products. While schools certainly hold very different priorities than corporations, their data needs might not be too dissimilar. An SLDS is, organizationally and structurally, very similar to a corporation in the data it maintains and accesses; the practice of MDM is a very relevant topic for consideration. Instead of discussing customers and products, an SLDS deals with students, test scores and staff. While there are obvious differences in the way a corporate entity and school system will operate, when it comes to managing data and maintaining an efficient, accurate database, MDM can provide many helpful best practices. MDM provides an established means for managing the quality issues that pervade every sector of the business economy, in many ways connecting or combining databases to create an SLDS is similar to a corporate acquisition or merger.

A strong MDM-based plan and governance structure can prevent or minimize several frequent and predictable issues that can arise in any SLDS. An efficiently managed MDM project will provide the dual benefit of enabling an organization to plan for long-term goals as well as deliver against short-term needs. An SLDS relying on MDM can promote a more efficient, less redundant and more agile system.

Less Data Redundancy

When merging records from two systems that deal with the same population, as with an SLDS, there will inevitably be overlap in records. Key data fields, such as student name and address, are collected repeatedly throughout the enterprise (in various arms of the system). Establishing business rules using MDM to dictate the reconciliation and merging process will lead to fewer duplicated records and greater consistency in data, saving time and resources in the future.

Improved Efficiency

When a user looks up a student record and sees multiple, possibly even conflicting records, how does he know which one is correct, or which one to update with new information? If the quality data practices are not in place, and there's no protocol on how records are merged or prioritized, there are obvious and inherent inefficiencies that prohibit users to work within the system. Users might not know how to update files such that their changes get accepted as the most accurate (a change of address, for instance.) These inefficiencies are prime examples of how an inefficient process can create high levels of user frustration and even prompt users to avoid using the data system altogether, and instances that should not exist in an SLDS governed by MDM.

Agility in the Face of Technological or Policy Change

One certainty in most fields is that the technology of today will soon be replaced by the technology of tomorrow. Organizations are constantly upgrading systems and standards, and rightly so. These changes cause a constant stream of changes that impact master data, a fact of business that will only serve to exacerbate any existing issues with data redundancy, inconsistency or process inefficiency. The idea that a data system should be in a format that can adapt to change is perhaps counterintuitive, though crucial to the system's sustainability. Governance is a key structure in MDM. Having Governance in place to address changes as they arise in a timely and prudent manner is important. MDM provides an SLDS with basic rules, processes and a governance structure to ensure the system continues to grow and adapt as time goes on.

INCORPORATING MDM PRINCIPLES IN YOUR SLDS

MDM is, essentially, a way for organizations to create one accurate version of the truth for each student's record. MDM involves exercises in data quality, data integration and data governance processes. The lines between the three areas aren't cut and dried;

there are many tasks that involve significant overlap in focus. For instance, data governance itself relies heavily on data quality. Data migrations involve data quality as well, and the data governance body will dictate the procedures and rules for the event. By putting processes and business rules in place to govern how each change is processed, MDM principles can lead to a high-quality SLDS for states to use in policy and educational decision making, with high levels of trust.

In this section, we show the ways to integrate MDM principles and practices into your SLDS project plan. In the planning stage, Governance will undertake data quality efforts to ensure the system's usefulness and ultimate success. Once the groundwork is laid, the system will be designed and implemented to meet stakeholders' needs. The established system will likely take one of two recommended forms—a federated data system or a centralized data warehouse architecture—and Governance will implement metadata rules and data dictionary. (These two architectures are discussed in detail in this chapter, and summarized in Chapter 2.) After the system is implemented, Governance will monitor the system, use the data and evaluate the policies and rules established in the beginning, judge their efficacy, and revise if needed.

In Chapter 2, we discussed several essential planning activities that are prerequisites to implementing an SLDS. Including MDM in the planning phases, with many of the discussions and decisions involving Governance, will create some additional planning activities.

Planning

Once the Governance of an SLDS has agreed upon MDM as its method of choice in regulating the data quality and integration process, the group will set out to define the scope of what they're integrating, and more precisely, they'll define *what* data is master data. Although MDM can provide much guidance for states in establishing business rules around data fields, it is not necessary nor advisable for states to take an MDM approach to all of the data they're maintaining. For instance, if a state adopts CEDS as its data dictionary, Governance would decide which elements are to be considered master data fields; it would be unfeasible to include the entire CEDS dictionary as master data. Typically, master data fields would include data like student identifying information and exit codes and other data points deemed important to have uniform across systems.

Also in this phase of the project, Governance will define the processes, agencies and sources of data, gaining a clear understanding of what is at stake. Within Governance, cross-functional teams should be established to take on individual processes and troubleshoot potentially difficult areas.

Data Quality

Put simply, the quality that goes into the system impacts the quality that comes out. We define data quality as: "The tools and processes that result in the creation of correct, complete and valid data that are required to support sound decision making."[1]

Data quality is a very important consideration for Governance when planning an SLDS. Attaining and maintaining a high level of data quality are to be ongoing tasks, and absolutely critical functions. "Implementing an LDS does not itself ensure higher data quality. However, it provides an opportunity to improve data quality by bringing errors and inconsistencies to light through the enterprise-wide integration of disparate silos."[2] So, better data quality system-wide is a result and a benefit of the establishment and proper functioning of Governance and SLDS; however, it requires attention and precision to achieve. Establishing and operating an SLDS isn't enough to improve data quality alone.

Data quality exercises are not optional and should not be treated as peripheral to an SLDS project. An SLDS populated with quality data is one that can attain all of the benefits and overcome the challenges discussed previously in Chapters 2 and 3. All of the potential uses of an SLDS—data-driven decisions, up-to-date student information to aid teachers in better helping students, policy decisions based on research—are predicated upon quality data. Educational leaders and policy makers are faced with tough decisions as America's education system continues to decline compared with other nations of the world. If users don't trust the data that are available to them, and if policy makers don't feel that the reports they're using to legislate educational policy are accurate, it's hard to see how the creation and implementation of the SLDS was worth it. Truly, having quality data with which to populate an SLDS is a crucial step.

There are several methods and concepts to be considered in this chapter that can inform Governance and help create data quality processes and standards for their agencies. Data quality exercises will need to be implemented at the source of the data (agency level), with some checks performed on the larger system. Governance will play a large role in the establishment and enforcement of these standards. Paying attention to data and valuing it as an asset can encourage stakeholders to take responsibility for their data quality. Additionally, data quality depends on a two-way communication pattern. For example, if an agency requests information that is stewarded by another agency, the requesting agency should report back to the data steward if errors or issues are found, with the source agency being responsible for making updates. This feedback loop is essential for the efficient functioning of this new data model. In this way, data quality results from data use.[3]

It's vital that the responsibility and motivation for quality data are spread across the system and its users: administrators, users and technical staff. Though there are simple system checks to run and troubleshoot common errors, many of the data quality issues will depend on the expertise and knowledge of school administrators and users and a thorough understanding of a specific process and procedure needed to create business rules that the technical staff can enforce and encode. Another key to efficiently maintaining data quality is to automate system checks wherever possible. Changes to a student's race, empty fields or fields with invalid formats should be spotted and remedied quickly using a standardized auditing procedure. These sorts of changes to data might be the result of human error, and system auditing procedures should be put into place to catch such errors.[4]

Ultimately, giving administrators and users the training and motivation to be vested in the data quality effort and help with its execution is how this can be effectively accomplished. Providing training and professional development to inform teachers how to spot and correct data errors and input consistent, quality data is important.[5] And further, facilitating the culture shift to one where data are used to support decisions and depended on in the classroom will reinforce the value of data, and, more specifically, data quality.

Design and Implement

During this phase of the project, Governance will drive the system design, and the technology team will develop it and get it up and running. During the design activities, creating workflows and rules for recurring access and feedback processes, and creating or choosing a data model for the system to subscribe to must be addressed. In an SLDS using MDM, each agency will use the same data dictionary for the data they track, describing each column or field (with information describing sources, uses and limitations on the field). As discussed in Chapter 3, CEDS publishes and maintains a data dictionary and a data model. The CEDS data model establishes the metadata and relationships between data fields, while the data dictionary can provide common definitions and understandings of the data to be collected and shared by each agency.

Once the basic infrastructure and rules of the system are established, the SLDS will be implemented. Data from multiple sources will be integrated, and business rules that have been created will be put to use. While many of the procedures that espouse MDM are very similar to a typical data project plan, a strong MDM implementation will have an especially solid foundation based on governance and focus on master data files.

Metadata Management

Often, LEAs and SEAs will be asked to report seemingly simple questions that quickly become complex and confusing, for instance, "List all of the middle schools in your state." It sounds simple, but with the differing structures of schools throughout the state it becomes harder to get a solid count. What exactly constitutes a middle school? Some schools hold seventh-, eighth-, and ninth-graders, some schools are K–6, and some are even K–12. Beyond that, if the SEA or LEA is asked to provide the number of students in middle school, does that mean only students in sixth to eight grades? What if they're taking some classes in different grades? Verification of data becomes very difficult, and the quality of data resulting from each LEA and SEA interpreting the definitions differently is clearly an issue. Metadata and universal definitions become important, even in order to answer simple questions.[6]

In a system where a metadata model is employed, the definition of each field is universally understood, making the aggregated result a verifiable number. There won't be uncertainty that one school district interpreted what a middle school student is and another district interpreted it differently. Metadata provides greater reliability and usability of the data.

Metadata management is a component of a master data management system. *Metadata* refers, broadly, to data about data. For any given data field in an SLDS, metadata can be tracked, associated and maintained. While master data management's purposes lie largely in data quality and interoperability, metadata management's purpose is mostly to organize and enable better usage of the data (though it does concern itself with interoperability and quality to some degree). "Metadata provide structured information that describes, explains, locates or otherwise makes it easier to retrieve, use or manage information."[7] Metadata management enables master data management to come to fruition.

Understandably, master data management and metadata management are two often-confused concepts. The key differences are shown in Figure 4.1, using an example from a restaurant as well as from a data system.

In an SLDS (as with most database systems), metadata can be business rules for the field, where the data originated, format restrictions, or previous definitions of the field, to give a few examples. Beyond being a way for instituting standards to ensure all contributors to the SLDS are giving compatible information, it is a way to tell the user more about the data than what is listed in the data field, providing more context. A field denoting a student's race or ethnicity is a good example of why this sort of information is necessary. There are many different ways to collect this information, and often different institutions or organizations will have different choices. There could be several ways to describe one student, depending on the choices given. In different systems, one child could be classified as: *American Indian, Native American, Cherokee* or *None of the Above.* Metadata for information received from multiple sources can help to reconcile these different choices and ensure each data field holds the correct response, based on the meanings of each field from contributing databases.

Figure 4.1   Master Data Management and Metadata Management

Considering the volumes of data that are available and stored in an SLDS, managing a data system without a metadata structure would simply be impractical. A central, authoritative metadata repository is an integral component in any SLDS.[8] Metadata is the key component to informed, contextualized use of data within the system.[9] In prior iterations of data systems, when no coordinated approach was set, what we term *metadata* might have been stored in the heads of those in each agency who were responsible for database upkeep. However, in the current technological environment and with the vast amounts of data and fields involved in an SLDS, more users and increasingly complex systems, it is simply unreasonable to operate this way going forward. Having a documented listing of the metadata, as well as a central, authoritative metadata repository is a crucial component to a state's ability to effectively contextualize the data in an SLDS. This imperative is even more critical in the climate of tight budgets and diminishing staff; without a strong and clear process dictated by Governance to the metadata, these efforts might be in danger when cuts are to be made.

Benefits of Metadata Management across the Enterprise

Tracking and maintaining robust metadata in a data system has several benefits.

Retrievability

Metadata management allows resources to be found when searched on relevant and related criteria. Though in the age of Google and advanced Internet searches this may sound simplistic, it is far from a given that databases will allow users to find what they're looking for easily. Associating metadata with data fields enables data elements to be grouped with other elements by various categories and functions, leading to more intelligent and easier system use.[10] In essence, the likelihood that the data will actually meet the users' needs goes up when metadata are incorporated into the system.[11] Metadata are contained in the data dictionary, allowing users to look up the business rules for specific fields, such as graduation rates or middle schools.

Context and Interoperability

Using agreed-upon metadata descriptors for a data element allows for each element to be understood in the same way by both people and machines across the differing hardware and software platforms.[12] It provides the means for improving the accuracy of data exchange among networked databases, reducing errors and making editing processes more efficient.[13] The anxiety felt among many agencies that their data will be misunderstood becomes a moot point entirely. When each agency has metadata for each data element it is using, more accurate interpretation is facilitated and greater trust can be placed in others' data. Data can be compared and true interoperability is achieved. Further, this universal understanding and context can be attained for more users, not just the most highly trained and technically proficient administrators of the system. Metadata provide context for users with various levels of expertise.[14]

From a practical standpoint, metadata management allows for code reusability across systems. One set of code from one database does not have to be rewritten to be used in other databases in the SLDS, saving the enterprise time and effort.

Archiving and Preserving

Most of the efforts being undertaken today involve cleaning data from the past to bring it up to today's standards; however, using metadata is a way for data systems to prime today's data for the future. By cataloging metadata associated with an element, you can ensure that the resource will survive and remain accessible and usable into the future, with less maintenance required for future transitions.

System Impact

Metadata management also provides an excellent framework for system-wide updates and alerts when data fields are impacted. "When someone wants a new field, what are the implications across systems? We can predict this now," Mike McGroarty, Michigan's SLDS manager, said after converting to a system that included metadata management.[15] If the address field in the data dictionary were being increased from 24 characters to 48 characters, this change would be preceded by an alert to all agencies to make this update to the way they use the field. It provides good-faith updates prior to changes to ensure each party is able to fully utilize the data and also that each agency's data remain intact. Using metadata to make richer data gives the overall enterprise the ability to make changes, informing its partnering agencies of the changes and impacts in a proactive way.

Implementing Metadata Management

To properly maintain metadata in your SLDS, you'll first need a metadata schema that sets the standards for the groupings, semantics and content definitions contained in the system.[16] This is a complex and technical process that most likely will be addressed by the software partner your state works with and Governance. It will impact the partner organizations to the SLDS and their data maintenance, but the legwork will likely be done by the software partner.

Luckily, metadata management principles and practices fold easily into the SLDS implementation process, with Governance overseeing many of the responsibilities of defining data fields' attributes and rules. It is also a component of master data management, aiding in its more efficient implementation and use. As we noted earlier, there are many important and invaluable benefits to be gained in utilizing metadata management, and it's our recommendation that states consider them when designing their SLDS.

Although defining and establishing protocol around your system's metadata can be a lengthy process, depending on the current state of data in your systems, it's a worthwhile undertaking for all of the reasons mentioned in this section. Providing context and sustainability to your data is a valuable insurance policy that the SLDS you're working hard to establish will be used and trusted well into the future. Investment in your SLDS's metadata infrastructure is sure to provide benefits to the system far outweighing the costs.[17]

Data System Architecture

MDM indicates centralized management of data, not necessarily centralized data. So, this method of managing data can be used with either of the two SLDS architectural approaches, the centralized data warehouse or the federated data system. MDM is often conflated with data warehousing, and while it can be involved in a data warehouse system, the two are different. This section will discuss the two prominent models for structuring an SLDS, outlining the differences and benefits of each. There are many concerns, limitations and differing goals that come into play when dealing with a group of stakeholders as large and dynamic as you're sure to face when setting up an SLDS and the two approaches detailed offer some flexibility depending on your state's needs and concerns. The centralized data warehouse and federated data system structures are the two most commonly utilized for SLDSs. When discussing the setup your state wants its LDS to take, keep in mind that a hybrid of the two structures outlined in this chapter is possible. Ensuring that the setup meets the technology needs for the SLDS is important. Both are customizable and no two states with the same architecture will have the exact same set of business rules and information flows.

Centralized Data Warehouse

One way to structure an SLDS is to combine each of the stakeholder databases into one *centralized data warehouse* (CDW). A data warehouse is a centralized repository of data, fed by various organizations. Within the CDW, there might be silos of protected information, automated processes to merge records and levels of access to protected or private information. A data warehouse is "a subject-oriented, integrated, time variant and non-volatile collection of data used in strategic decision making," as Bill Inmon defined it in the 1980s.[18] This definition is still widely regarded today.

A CDW serves as the facilitator to turn organizational data into information by delivering a common view of the data. The CDW provides the infrastructure and framework to unify data from varying geographies and of varying quality levels and provides a unified view of all the data a system holds.[19] Getting all of the data in one centralized location is a first step to surveying those data and using them to inform action. The data in a CDW are set up to be used by each agency that contributes to it, and therefore are designed to be compatible with each form of analytical technology used within the organization. The CDW serves all of its constituents, rather than each individual data mart serving as an autonomous producer and consumer of data.[20]

A CDW can grow over time. When the CDW is implemented, it will be set up from the beginning to enable huge proportional growth to accommodate the influx of data to come over time. Having access to a high volume of historical data in a very efficient manner is a defining characteristic of a CDW. Additionally, it is recommended best practice to design a CDW to handle change and load large amounts of data quickly. Facilitating such system upgrades is worth it, as it puts the CDW in the position to grow over time and continue to function well under changing needs.[21]

This architecture is simpler than a federated data system in many ways, allowing for one owner of all of the records and smoother business processes surrounding the data. A CDW eliminates the need for data silos at each organization, thus dissolving the responsibility of ownership from the source of the data. The agencies, in effect, outsource the maintenance of their data, freeing up time to use and analyze data. Having one record in one place creates one single version of the truth, making data easier to maintain and more accurate in reporting and analysis. In this way, having all state data stored and maintained centrally diminishes the collective burden of responsibility on each stakeholding group. A CDW may take a greater upfront investment of time and resources, but over time can better handle system growth and change.

There are many intricacies to setting up a CDW-based SLDS. While it is simpler than formulating a federated data system for all parties, there are many common pitfalls that might make implementing a data warehouse challenging. A common mistake states make when setting up a CDW SLDS is underestimating the time necessary to effectively plan the system, and not investing enough resources in the data warehouse. Shortchanging the early phases can lead to a subpar design, with the end result being a system that meets only a fraction of the needs it was designed to meet. Planning and negotiating with partner agencies about business rules, privacy standards and system compatibility can be taxing processes, but they are necessary to the ultimate success of the system.

Federated Data System

Sometimes, it is not feasible to completely merge all of the databases in a vast system to make the state's LDS. Be it security and privacy concerns or technological and logistical concerns, there are many valid reasons that states might seek an option that allows each party to maintain its own, autonomous database while still sharing data to the system when requested from peer agencies and researchers. This second option is known as a *federated data system*.

A federated data system provides for the necessities of a common database, while still allowing for each agency to maintain ownership of its data. Data ownership and maintenance can be important issues among state agencies, making this system a good compromise (without sacrificing any functionality). It also places value upon the time, resources and creative energy that have gone into creating an agency's current database solution, not forcing each to abandon all that it has established and embrace a common architecture. While certain changes to allow interoperability and process compatibility will be inevitable, most federated data systems allow partner agencies to retain a large portion of their established system. Allowing for existing, compatible databases, software and processes to be folded into an SLDS rather than mandating that they accept new technology is a boon for agencies with good current data processes, few resources and decreasing budgets. It can also aid in quicker implementation.

A federated data system allows for databases to share limited data among each other while remaining autonomous.[22] For a federated data system to be operational, a defined set of contributory agencies is needed; a centralized data broker, a federal data dictionary to ensure interoperability of data between partner agencies and a protocol of import and export procedures are important prerequisites. The federation of partner agencies will make their data available to other members, while receiving indirect access to data from the federation (through the data broker).[23]

In the center of a federated data system sits a data broker that all of the partner agencies are connected to and that transparently connects the partner agencies to one another. The databases may be geographically decentralized. A protocol is established to regulate the process for reporting data from several partner agencies. Commonly, reports are channeled through the data broker hub, with student records sent through the system, deidentified and returned to the requester. Duplicate records are merged and the requester receives the information without having to request it from each agency, a labor-intensive (and highly inefficient) process. In this way, a requester could receive data from any number of agencies, almost as it would in a centralized data warehouse setup.

Virginia's SLDS uses the federated data system architecture. Its SLDS follows a very basic step-by-step process to safeguard all parties' data and security while providing federated partners with their requests.

Step 1: Agencies deidentify data and apply hash algorithm with common seed to common data elements.

Step 2: Using the hash, third-party matches records, strips hash and assigns unique identifier.

Step 3: Records delivered to requester.

Through this system, with two safeguards in place to protect private student data, no receiving party can match the linked records back to identifiable data.[24]

Setting up a system that works for all partners in the federation is a challenge, and a strong planning and requirements gathering process is an important first step toward establishing a federated data–based SLDS. One issue Governance and stakeholders will have to address early on is the protocol for system change. Once the standards and policies are agreed upon, additional vendors can be used by the sector as long as they adhere to the structures set forth by Governance. While technological change is the rule rather than the exception in the future of educational data, with a data warehouse, there is one system to maintain and adapt if a change occurs. With a federated data structure, one partner changing its system can impact the entire SLDS.

Integrating MDM into a federated data system is slightly different than in a CDW. While each state charts its own setup and processes surrounding updates to master data and how those changes are communicated to the agency databases, one option is for the central data broker to hold only the master records and push updates when changes are made. It is possible, and advisable, to use MDM with a federated approach, as the need for one authoritative data file for each student does not change based on the system's setup.

Evaluate, Monitor and Use

The final stage is the ongoing process of evaluating and controlling the data system using MDM principles. This involves the enforcing of business rules created by Governance, evaluation of the reliability of the system, and refining of business rules to suit the system's use. Stakeholders can begin using data from the system for analysis and to drive decision making.

Data Stewards

A concept that is frequently considered a best practice in an MDM data system is that of a data steward. Using this process, established in the planning phase, Governance can appoint one steward to each data element, making that person responsible for the data quality associated with that element. So, rather than having an entire group of users responsible for all of the data their agency is contributing, a data steward would be appointed to each domain (and all the data and fields contained within it). The data steward would be able to hone his expertise and better utilize his time on one area, and rely on the specialization of others within the peer agencies to manage the rest of the data fields. Often, in an SLDS, one agency can be identified as the authoritative supplier for one dataset. For instance, one group might commonly supply the high school graduation data and a member of this group could be appointed the data steward for it since they deal with it most often. Leaders within each agency who exhibit a subject-matter expertise or exceptional knowledge about certain fields are excellent candidates to be data stewards.

In practice, this method of data quality maintenance involves the orchestration of system checks and alerts. In a CDW, the data stewards would run reports (or view automated periodical reports) on the data fields for which they're responsible, enabling them to spot potential issues as they're forming rather than when they become a large problem. Data stewards monitor data after integrations to ensure the system is acting according to the business rules established at the onset of the SLDS planning, and further, that the business rules make sense in practice.

One of the best practices mentioned in the section discussing data quality detailed a feedback loop in which users of the data would report issues in data quality they spot. Data stewards, in this process, would be the resolvers of these issues. When issues are found, either from a user or through a system check, an alert can be put out to the data steward and attention drawn to the issue.

This method for spreading responsibility and accountability evenly among stakeholders is a best practice. As each state's LDS will take its own shape due to the unique factors that influence its agencies and data, the data stewardship process is a dynamic one that can change over time and depending on system concerns. We recommend establishing data stewards to promote greater data quality, agency investment in the system and accountability among agencies.

CONCLUSION

There is no best way to achieve a functioning SLDS; each state has its own set of unique requirements and circumstances that will shape its SLDS. MDM is a key concept that should inform your state's planning and organizational decisions, providing guidance on dealing with data quality, metadata management and system architecture. Implementing all of the processes detailed in the chapter is not essential to your system's success; it is certainly possible to choose priority strategies that will have the greatest impact on your system's design and function. It is, however, a best practice to include discussions and a high level of attention to these principles and practices when considering your SLDS setup and processes.

NOTES

1. Information Management, http://www.information-management.com/channels/data-quality.html (accessed April 10, 2012).
2. NCES, *Traveling Through Time: The Forum Guide to Longitudinal Data Systems* (Alexandria, VA: ED Publications, 2010).
3. Ibid.
4. Ibid.
5. Ibid.
6. Karl Pond, personal interview (June 2012).
7. National Forum on Education Statistics, *Forum Guide to Metadata: The Meaning Behind Education Data* (Washington, DC: U.S. Department of Education, National Center for Education Statistitcs, 2009), http://nces.ed.gov/pubs2009/2009805.pdf.
8. NCES, *Traveling Through Time*.
9. Ibid.
10. National Information Standards Organization, *Understanding Metadata* (Bethesda, MD: NISO Press, 2004).
11. NCES, *Traveling Through Time*.
12. National Information Standards Organization, *Understanding Metadata*.
13. National Forum on Education Statistics, *Forum Guide to Metadata*.

14. Ibid.

15. Mike McGroarty, Michigan SLDS manager, personal interview (Georgia Mariani), November 18, 2011.

16. National Information Standards Organization, *Understanding Metadata*.

17. National Forum on Education Statistics, *Forum Guide to Metadata*.

18. W. H. Inmon, *Buliding the Data Warehouse*, 3rd ed. (New York: John Wiley & Sons, 2001).

19. Claudia Imhoof, Nicolas Galemmo, and Jonathan G. Geiger, *Mastering Data Warehouse Design: Relational and Dimensional Techniques* (Indianapolis: Wiley Publishing, 2003).

20. Ibid.

21. Ibid.

22. Dennis Heimbinger and Dennis McLeod, "A Federated Architecture for Information Management," *ACM Transactions on Office Information Systems* 3, no. 3 (July 1985): 253–278.

23. Ibid.

24. State Support Team (NCES), "P-20W Federated Data Systems," PowerPoint presentation (November 16, 2011).

CHAPTER **5**

Florida Case Study: The Up- and Downside of Being the First

lorida's statewide longitudinal data system (SLDS) is one of the oldest in the country, being functional since 2003 and currently ranking highly among state systems. The Data Quality Campaign (DQC) rates states based on 10 elements that excellent SLDSs should have to be functional and maximized; Florida meets all 10 criteria. The DQC also rates states based on 10 actions, measuring how the state utilizes and maintains its SLDS; Florida has 8 of the 10 actions (no state has yet reached all 10). What's more, "Florida was the first in the nation to implement all of the ten essential elements."[1] The DQC's rating scale is seen as a good measure of systems industry-wide, and Florida is near the top by most standards.

Florida has been the beneficiary of several federal grants to establish and enrich its SLDS. Since 2005, Florida has received over $14 million from NCES and Race to the Top for various projects relating to its system. It is currently in the process of revamping and redesigning its SLDS (statewide longitudinal data systems) to make it more accessible, more up-to-date and filled with high-quality data. It's a leading-edge system; however, Kit Goodner, who oversees Florida's SLDS, says good-naturedly, "If it were perfect, we wouldn't be redoing it."

Florida is in a unique situation in that it has a great longitudinal data system, but outmoded software and processes that need updating. Federal grants and copious longitudinal data enabled it to get off the ground early and lead the nation in SLDS; however, this early leader status poses some developmental and funding challenges.

FLORIDA'S SLDS

Florida's SLDS holds longitudinal data dating back to 1995, with some agencies contributing much older data. It tracks 2.5 million students. Florida doesn't currently map to CEDS, though the state is using the CEDS data alignment tool to get there in the near future.

Florida uses a centralized data warehouse architecture for its SLDS. When the system was established in 2003, it was a logical setup (with agreements already existing with many data sources, such as the Department of Labor, the military and the Department of Health). "Because it was one of the first to step into the realm, I don't think there was a lot of discussion in going another route," Gene Kovacs said regarding the architecture of Florida's SLDS. Kovacs is the current CIO of the Florida University Board of Governors and was involved as a senior analyst for the Florida College System when the warehouse was deployed. With vast amounts of student unit records at each agency, merging them together in one shared database was an easy decision. There wasn't immediate buy-in and enthusiasm from the involved agencies. Kovacs notes that it took a while until everyone was on board, until the system started giving back quality data that proved its worth.

Currently, the SLDS receives data from and makes data available to: K–12 (comprised of 72 districts), Florida colleges (28 institutions), technical centers (more than 20 institutions), and the state university system (12 universities). Goodner estimates that 70 percent of the data in the SLDS comes from these main feeder systems. Beyond these primary stakeholders, there are some workforce components currently included, though more are set to be included in projects under current grants.

The SLDS has had a fractured history, epitomizing the political forces that can impact the development of a system like this. Shortly after the SLDS was established, then-Governor Jeb Bush realigned the Department of Education in 2001, combining K–20 and all higher education under one umbrella and dissolving the Board of Regents that had previously governed the state university system. This union wasn't meant to be and in 2003, a constitutional amendment was passed to establish a Board of Governors to manage the university system's unique needs. All of this organizational change was going on as the system was trying to establish its processes, data quality policies and system. It's rare that an SLDS would have a smooth and simple path to completion, but Florida's was particularly rocky.

RENOVATING WHAT EXISTS USING FEDERAL GRANTS

In discussing Florida's processes and systems, it seems there isn't much that is not under construction under the umbrella of NCES and RTTT grant funds. Part of the up- and downside of being one of the first in the nation to have an SLDS means that after being up and running for nearly a decade, it's time for the next iteration.

The amount of data in the Florida SLDS set it apart from other SLDSs. They've been "collecting unit record student data for over 25 years." Kovacs notes in conversations with other states, "You talk to some states and they've just started (implementation)." Florida is ahead in this area, at the forefront of the SLDS movement. However, the primary factor that sets Florida's system apart from others is also one of the primary factors that make its work more difficult. Having a mature longitudinal data system is a mixed bag. "Being at the forefront, you start going down a road that no one's ever trod before," Kovacs notes, and it's inevitable that mistakes will be made and certain decisions won't hold up over time. As a 10-year-old system nearing the end of its federal funding stream, Florida's reality is a lot different than it was as a brand-new system, when it was the beneficiary of numerous federal grants and accolades.

It's an iterative process, like any large-scale technology project. After 10 years of system development and use, it's going to be time to reevaluate some things and address unforeseen issues that have arisen. This is a natural part of the process, but one that isn't necessarily financially supported by SLDS grants. Kovacs notes that the funding sources that were integral in getting Florida's SLDS off the ground will likely go to new systems, and demand results proving that Florida has achieved its goals with the money it did receive.

This is where the mixed blessing of being among the first SLDSs comes into play. "If you started fresh, what would you do?" Kovacs says. "Maybe there would have been some different decisions and different things that would have happened." Some decisions that were made and implemented years ago might not have been the best, but changing them becomes harder and harder, Kovacs notes. And as the funding dries up, it's harder to drum up the support to make changes that can improve the system as a whole.

Kovacs noted that "developing operational data systems primarily with grant funds makes overall strategic planning difficult." The federal grant proposal applications are time sensitive and sometimes necessarily truncate the planning cycle. Each grant also has its own set of requirements, areas of emphasis, and restrictions that must be followed, creating a situation where midstream changes can be difficult to initiate. While federal funding is a boon to states in setting up these systems, in many ways the process itself is limiting and poses challenges. And states must be cognizant that the grant periods will inevitably end, and "once grant funds are gone an entity must be ready to provide the resources to continue the operations or completion of the projects," according to Kovacs.

Florida's Office of Accountability, Research and Measurement within the Department of Education currently oversees 14 projects relating to the SLDS upgrades, under three separate federal grants (2009 NCES SLDS grant, 2009 ARRA and RTTT). There are a lot of improvements to Florida's system on elements that are either insufficient or outdated. The combined efforts of all of the changes make for a huge undertaking in a relatively short period of time, though that's necessary to meet the conditions of the grants. That's one of the difficulties with the grant and award system: high expectations and tight deadlines.

Data Quality

To get updated data from its LEAs, the system facilitates survey-based submission periods several times throughout the year. During these times, they essentially open up the source systems that eventually feed new data into the data warehouse. These submission periods vary in length and, once closed, the state will certify the data, do a quality analysis and move them into the warehouse. Updates occur on a more-or-less ongoing basis, with about eight submissions per year for the K–12 sector. Florida colleges and technical centers use a similar process, with several submission periods throughout the year (including personnel, financial and facilities data collections). These collections from educational data sources were in place for years prior to the creation of the data warehouse. The existing system is not a transactional system, which is what Florida is moving to. The new setup, which is currently being architected, will allow for more frequent submission, leading to more accurate data and analysis. It will also allow for greater flexibility in how districts can submit their data.

One key challenge that states face when they accept a data warehouse model is the unknown quality of data that each agency will contribute. The current system offers a very manual and labor-intensive data quality verification process to ensure that the data being sent into the system are valid. The system renovations will include a more comprehensive and instantaneous data quality process, involving a feedback loop to the data source. This feedback is essential in curbing the prevalence of data quality issues; if agencies are aware of the issues, they can address them and prevent further occurrence.

Unique Identifier System

Florida's unique identifier (UID) system is more complex than most. Student records are matched using local identifiers that are then matched to an internal identifier, which is not disclosed to districts and schools. Districts each have their own system of establishing an identifier to use for each student (some even use Social Security numbers). Once the initial student record data are established, an internal identifier is established and linked, although Goodner notes that it is possible (though unlikely) for two students to have the same identifier. A common UID is highly preferable to a local student identifier, providing a more seamless system and higher efficacy. For instance, if a student moves to a new school within the state, it's likely that he will have a different identifier, adding steps to the process and more opportunities for error. Florida's efforts to establish a more efficient UID system are a big part of making the SLDS more accurate.

Researcher Access Process

Providing access to the data in the data warehouse is something Florida is also in the process of revamping. Currently, sharing data with a researcher is a very manual process. The researcher will submit a data request and "we'll find a way to get it to you," says Goodner. While they have several methods to accomplish this, all involve a person orchestrating it. The new system is set to involve more automation, providing access to the data requested (and authorized) using data marts and cubes. A data mart is usually created based on specific business needs of various user groups, including datasets that are likely to be queried or desired. Data marts pull in raw data from the data warehouse and provide controlled access to the data for specified user roles. Online analytical processing (OLAP) cubes are built on top of data marts, and are assembled using hierarchy classifications for the data, enabling easier querying and the ability to aggregate data or drill down to the information the user is looking for. Data marts and cubes also provide role- and row-level security, making the access process simpler and more secure for researchers. It also offers functionality to make the data useful for researchers. "Part of what we're doing is to greatly improve access to data," Goodner says of the changes.

As part of a project associated with Florida's RTTT grant, they plan to include business intelligence (BI) tools, like dashboards and reports, to enhance the usability and usefulness of the data in the warehouse. BI technologies have made a big impact on many business industries and, indeed, technologies like this hold tremendous promise for educational systems to increase efficiency and usability. Overall in the system upgrades and renovations, Goodner notes that "probably what governs us the most is data quality and data access. Once we solve those issues, I think that we will consider ourselves fairly successful."

Creating a Formal Data Governance Body

One anomaly in Florida's leading-edge SLDS is that it has no data governance board to dictate policy and data practices and make key decisions. They are currently in the process of forming a data governance body, as a grant-funded project. Issues have arisen in which having assigned roles and responsibilities under an official governance structure would have benefited the state, including metadata management, a complex issue requiring an informed and nuanced approach.

Though there was no formal Governance in the establishment of the SLDS nearly 10 years ago, there was collaboration among the partner agencies, and each agency conducts its own Governance to ensure its data quality and policies. The meetings and discussions were helpful in establishing the system and its processes; however, the economy impacted the sustainability of such collaborations. Several departments saw severe cutbacks at various points since 2003, which required cutting back staff and time available for fostering the implementation communication efforts. They eventually fizzled out, according to Kovacs; however, it seems they had enough time to make an impact on the structure of the system. Having the official structure is important, and Florida sees it as such, even after the SLDS is established and operative.

CONCLUSION

Florida's is a system that leads the charge in SLDS acceptance and implementation. The state's renovation of its existing system illustrates how the changing technologies and resources are making possible an even more efficient system than could be imagined when it was first started 10 years ago. These sorts of upgrades, expansions and improvements are to be expected in a system of this magnitude. It's also a conflicting reality with the federal funding that flows to SLDSs; the money that establishes and enhances them will eventually end. One thing Florida's experience plainly shows is the importance of establishing support at the state legislature level, either in the form of matching or ongoing funding for after the federal grant period is over, to ensure the future of the system. Logically, if a state is spending millions of dollars to invest in software systems, training and infrastructure to accommodate an SLDS, the state won't want the system to be gone in three years. It will want educated staff members to make it better and sustain it over time. These issues must be addressed so the future of the system isn't in jeopardy. Florida's current state of change and upgrade are indicative of growth and enhancement, which will only serve to make its SLDS more efficient and useful in its educational system.

NOTES

Interviews in this chapter conducted by the author with: Keith Goodner, Assistant Deputy Commissioner for Accountability, Research and Measurement, SLDS program director, Florida Department of Education, June 14, 2012; and Gene Kovacs, CIO of the Florida University Board of Governors, formerly a senior analyst for the Florida College System during SLDS development and setup, July 30, 2012.

1. Gina Jordan, "Florida among the Leaders in Improving Education Data," StateImpact, http://stateimpact.npr.org/florida/2011/12/01/florida-among-the-leaders-in-improving-education-data/ (accessed February 2, 2012).

CHAPTER 6

Michigan Case Study: SLDS—a Tool for Reinventing the Economy

In recent years, Michigan has undergone an economic shift. For decades, the state's economy thrived because of the American automotive industry, with high school and college graduates easily landing and keeping good jobs in auto factories and associated industries. As the American auto industry deteriorated, this has impacted Michigan's economy immensely. Over the last decade, Detroit has lost 25 percent of its population.[1] Looking to the future, Michigan sees the need to reinvent its economy. In the educational sector, this leads to a renewed focus on the education Michigan's students are receiving to ensure they're fully equipped to usher in a new era of prosperity for the state.

"It's really a statewide effort right now on making sure we're understanding how and at what pace we're preparing students for a better future. Michigan was a highly automotive-driven, manufacturing state. We're still very proud of that in our state, but it's not as predominant as it was in years past," said Tom Howell, director of Michigan's Center for

Educational Performance and Information (CEPI). As the manager of the state's statewide longitudinal data system (SLDS) project, Howell has been part of the project since the beginning. Many of Michigan's efforts center on enhancing science, technology, engineering and math curricula, with that sector of the economy booming and holding a potential bright spot in Michigan's future. "The automotive industry is still very important to us, but it's not as robust of an industry as it used to be, so we really have to look to other opportunities that require students to become more astute in the math, science and technology skill sets," says Howell.

Michigan's economic reinvention is excellent motivation for initiatives that have aided in its SLDS development and implementation. As the recipient of three NCES (National Center for Educational Statistics) SLDS grants, Michigan has invested years of time and energy planning and implementing its SLDS, which will soon be available to classroom teachers and school administrators. Though it is still in the implementation phase, the system is already providing value to Michigan's educational system through partnerships like the Career and College Ready Initiative.

MICHIGAN'S SLDS: MOVING BEYOND COMPLIANCE

When NCES started offering grants in 2006 to get states to set up statewide longitudinal data systems, Michigan was all ears. It had spent years and years maturing in the way it gathered and stored student data to make compliance reporting simpler. All of the federal data processes and changes are "costly, cumbersome and difficult, both for the state and the schools," according to Howell. And all of that effort was aimed only at doing government-mandated reporting; they weren't able to give anything meaningful back to educators that might affect their realities in the classroom. So when the opportunity came to set up an SLDS that might address their complex compliance needs as well as offer the opportunity to dive deeper into the data and provide them to their teachers, leaders in Michigan's educational system were on board with the mission and applied for the grant. "We thought it very important to focus on turning that compliance data into something much more actionable and much more useful," Howell notes. "We wanted to move beyond compliance."

"We're deliberately going about building a system that answers relevant and timely questions. The complexity in the approach is it takes longer to establish a system; in the end it'll be more powerful and much quicker for folks to use once it's on the ground," Howell says. To date, Michigan has received three SLDS grants (two under NCES's SLDS program and one given under the American Recovery and Reinvestment Act) to build the capacity for and access portals to its longitudinal data. In total, Michigan has received over $19 million for its SLDS from 2006 to 2009.[2] As deadlines to prove achievement of deliverables promised on these grants loom, the state is under pressure to get the system functioning and providing data to stakeholders.

The System

Michigan's SLDS most closely resembles a centralized data warehouse (as discussed in Chapter 4), though Howell notes that in Michigan they like to conceptualize it as a "data mart." Michigan's system is comprised of a large data mart and a series of OLAP (Online Analytical Processing) cubes. Results from the system are returned through a public portal (mischooldata.org) that will allow public and tiered access to users depending on their credentials. Howell notes that the data mart they've established is more complex than a centralized data warehouse. "We do not just move raw data into these data structures. There are computations, and there's a lot of work that goes on in transforming that data into meaningful information that we store," he says.

The system currently houses around 3.5 million student records, adding over 100,000 annually. It's currently a P20 system, incorporating all state-funded preschools, K–12, and all postsecondary institutions (public and private). There are working plans to include workforce data in the system in the coming years. Its P20 system holds records dating back to 2003 (K–12) and 2009 (postsecondary). Michigan maps to CEDS (Common Education Data Standards), though it's not officially CEDS compliant at this point. CEPI pulls data from over 850 districts and 45 public colleges and universities, many using very different local student data systems. The diversity of local software options used by the education agencies makes CEDS compliance a serious undertaking. To account for the many and varied formats of data received, CEPI takes the data and maps them to CEDS in its metadata repository. This enables greater interoperability of the data and opens the door for multistate data exchange in the future.

Since 2001, Michigan has utilized a unique identification code (UIC) for K–12 students. Since 2009, preschool and public postsecondary institutions also use the UICs to connect their student records. Michigan has extended its UIC to career and technical education programs, special education programs, adult education, migrant education and all testing systems in the state. Additionally, Michigan has extended the UIC to many private school students, with the UIC used as the common identifier on all state assessments. "We've been working pretty hard to establish that the common identifier is used across all the education programs administered by the state," Howell said.

Under state law, Michigan is not allowed to collect data that are not required by a state or federal statute. Therefore, the SLDS does not collect items like transactional data. The preschool and K–12 data are updated three times annually. Following those collections, they'll be processed and the database will be up to date by 45 days post-collection. The goal is to get the turnaround time down to 30 days without jeopardizing data quality. Postsecondary data are updated once annually. Staff and teacher data, once those data structures are established, will be updated twice a year.

Involving Stakeholders: Shared Goals, Shared Responsibility

Though CEPI is the primary agency responsible for steering and implementing Michigan's SLDS efforts, it requires investment from stakeholders and the political will of many to accomplish the task. Engaging and involving stakeholders is a crucial facet to keeping energy and enthusiasm up on the project.

Most states have a body that oversees public education from preschool through postsecondary education, but Michigan does not have one. In Michigan, several agencies share in the management of the educational system. So, entering into a long-term educational project was daunting without an authoritative organization to oversee it. Additionally, the state constitution establishes the state colleges and universities as autonomous and independent of the state (even though they are publicly funded). With so many independent entities and no higher authority, Michigan's educational community was understandably anxious about embarking on a project like this one, where getting all vital members to the table and in agreement would be essential.

To plan, implement and oversee the P20 system, the governor appointed the P20 Longitudinal Data System Advisory Council under an executive order. It is comprised of stakeholders who contribute and use data from the SLDS, as well as those with an interest or expertise in the project who are not data consumers. The committee is made up of representatives from the state educational agencies, the workforce development agency, the labor and regulation agencies, the Treasury Department, the technology, management and budget agency (state CIO and state budget director), the Early Childhood Investment Corporation, private research firms, Michigan's four-year state universities and community colleges, and representatives from a sampling of K–12 school districts. It was important to Michigan from the beginning to have a variety of voices at the table, including those without vested interests and politically driven motivations. The breadth of viewpoints and supply of independent voices that Michigan has populated its Governance Board with is truly a model to emulate.

Within the P20 Council, there are workgroups that form to address issues related to subsets of the data. For instance, there are workgroups focused on K–12 data, and issues involving workforce data. This sort of approach recognizes that governance is not a single-tier issue and there are tactical issues that different subgroups might address more adeptly, with their differing expertise.

The P20 Council, then, facilitated the communication that helped Michigan overcome its lack of institutional authority. There was (and is) a nearly constant conversation, discussing how the data will be managed and how they will be leveraged and used to inform all levels of the educational pipeline. A useful byproduct of this effort and collaboration is that agencies became more aware of how their inputs and outputs were impacting each other and of how they could improve on their programs. For instance, through an effort to better understand college readiness, postsecondary data were used to shed light on the level of remediation and rework that their students needed upon enrolling in higher education. When K–12 institutions could see how well (or how poorly) their students were performing based on the preparation their own institutions had provided, it gave a better understanding of how the inputs have resulted in quality output—producing a student who's ready for the next level of education. Conveying through communication and the P20 Council's work that stakeholders have shared goals and mutual benefit in the project has been a strength of Michigan's SLDS effort. "We simply have overcome some of our challenges by working closely together, making sure everyone is at the table and making a true partnership in terms of what we're trying to accomplish," Howell said of Michigan's approach.

Given this success in collaboration among government and private agencies, Howell advises other states to pay close attention to the stakeholders. Though it adds an extra level of complexity, constant communication is vital. The consequences of assuming everyone is on board can be major. "If you have a small set of stakeholders that don't understand what you're doing, they will fight you. You have to make sure everyone's involved and everyone's at the table, sharing in what you're trying to accomplish."

Engineered to Last: Roll with the Changes

Mention data sharing and SLDSs and one of the first concerns most will share is privacy. Michigan was no exception to this rule. "Privacy and confidentiality are huge issues in our state," Howell says. This shared concern shaped their SLDS and the privacy measures built into it. Additionally, there are federal regulations (FERPA, most notably) and regulations from the U.S. Department of Education restricting how certain data are handled and accessed. The software system that Michigan contracted to engineer and facilitate its SLDS (SAS) allowed for flexible definitions, accommodating current laws and the inevitable future laws. "The advantage of using SAS for our small agency was that it was a really creative approach to getting around the constant need to rely on a technology company to code and recode every time a rule or regulation or data point changed over time," Howell said. Retaining a level of agility in the technology is vital to surviving in the long term, realizing that the "data marts and warehouses are not going to be static—they'll have to be adjusted over time." Finding an intuitive and flexible software solution that allows for maintenance to be done in-house saves the state time and money.

A major component of Michigan's SLDS project is making the longitudinal data available to the public and to researchers, which certainly puts a fine point on confidentiality of certain elements. The tools from the software solution made it simple to extract and publish certain information to the Internet, making it available for public consumption. Including the researchers who can help to analyze and interpret results from the data contained in the SLDS is something Michigan included in its project as well. It has established a security model for the online portal involving a three-tiered access system. It's still being developed and implemented, but the goal is to have three levels of access. Depending on the researcher's credentials and needs, he would have access to deidentified, anonymized or scrambled data sets.

The Approach: Start with the Basics and Expand

Michigan's approach to building its SLDS has been pragmatic and deliberate from the beginning. "We're trying to stay focused on the core data being student-centric and then expanding out," says Howell. An SLDS can seem overwhelming; when states look at lists of data to pull in from dozens of sources, it can quickly become too big to handle. Michigan's approach has been to start with a set of core student data and expand to more data and more useful processes as the system matures. "So, while we're working on providing more and more discrete-level access to that student-centric data we'll also be adding data sources (like staffing and workforce) and increased functionality," he says. Since the system has been in the works for several years, CEPI is beginning to branch out in the data it is ready to add, and broader access to the system will soon be authorized.

While the SLDS is able to add value and functionality in early stages through providing reporting capability (all federal EDEN reporting is completed using the system), it is still incomplete and not a fully functional SLDS. At this point it is actually two separate entities—a disconnected SLDS and a public-facing information portal. "The vision is that the SLDS will eventually feed all the data to the public portal," Howell says. The reality is that getting the information cleaned, organized and locked down to feed to the portal is a time-consuming process that involves most of the SLDS team.

Currently, the Michigan SLDS lacks the capacity to push data to teachers, one of the most anticipated and most useful functions of an SLDS. "We do have a distributed security model in our portal that we are working to enhance so that we can distribute that security out to the districts and further allow them to provide more discrete-level access to their employees," Howell notes. It's a step in the direction of teacher-level access. But that doesn't stop teachers and districts from being anxious to receive the data the SLDS holds, which is both good and bad news for Howell and for CEPI. It is taking a little longer than expected to provide end-to-end longitudinal data to stakeholders, and the stakeholders are anxiously anticipating the data. On all levels of the P20 continuum, Howell says, there are frequent requests for data that are just not ready yet. "We're a very small agency," he says, and the system is being developed according to a set plan. "We're getting there, but it's just going to take some time."

Realizing that trying to focus in too many directions with limited staff can be quickly overtaxing and problematic for getting anything accomplished at all, Howell keeps CEPI focused on establishing the core student data records, with an eye on expanding the distribution methods in the future. Adding "information on teacher effectiveness and information on our teacher-prep programs and building data sets that help the taxpayers understand their investment in public education whether it be preschool or K–12 or postsecondary education" are all in the works while the core system is being established. "We're going down a couple different paths at the same time."

CAREER AND COLLEGE READY INITIATIVE: HOW LONGITUDINAL DATA CAN INFORM THE DISCUSSION

Michigan's state economy had been largely dependent on the automotive industry in years past, and recent economic changes have made the future of new high school graduates different from what it was in the past. While in the past a student in Michigan could graduate high school, be trained in a technical field and have a good job in the automotive sector, today's economic success is dependent on different skills. A college education or, minimally, a high school diploma is now seen as vital in Michigan's economic future.

In recent years, there has been an increased focus on helping Michigan's students become career and college ready. Like many states, Michigan's educational system has started to focus on science and technology fields, where it believes there's an economic opportunity for the state. As part of this shift, Michigan sees it as vital that the state educate the next generation of scientists and technologists and ensure the credentials they're earning are top-notch.

In April 2006, then-Governor Jennifer Granholm signed into law a comprehensive and rigorous update to Michigan's statewide graduation requirement: the Michigan Merit Curriculum (MMC). Prior to the update, the state only required that students take one semester of civics to receive a high school diploma. Though many school districts adopted additional local requirements for graduating, there was no consistency across the state and, therefore, little comparability in high school diploma value among Michigan's graduates.[3] The MMC updated the statewide graduation requirements to be among the most rigorous in the country and ushered in a new focus on the career and college readiness of Michigan's students.

After the MMC was established, there was great interest in evaluating its effectiveness. The Michigan Consortium for Educational Research (MCER) was established to study the Michigan Merit Curriculum and the Michigan Promise Scholarship (MPS). This five-year, $6 million partnership between the University of Michigan, Michigan State University and state educational agencies (including CEPI, Michigan Department of Education) is evaluating the new curriculum and its effects on students' readiness for life after high school using longitudinal data. It is also helping Michigan accomplish one of its deliverables under the NCES grant: to develop a prototype for partnering between states, LEAs (local educational agencies) and universities for research and evaluation purposes. MCER, by all accounts, "could result in a more powerful mechanism for studying, analyzing and recording information about our public institutions," according to Howell.

This consortium provides a tremendous service to the state of Michigan in the early phases of development of its SLDS. Few new SLDSs have the opportunity to involve researchers and academia in the state's educational data in the early stages. This serves as a sort of "pilot research collaborative," giving key insight into the researcher perspective and needs for longitudinal data. Though MCER isn't formally involved in the SLDS implementation (they're not involved in data governance or policy decisions), their findings are helping to shape the SLDS setup. And, of course, MCER also provides the evaluation mechanism for the MMC and MPS. One often-noted argument against asking research-driven questions is the lack of time and energy among LEAs and SEAs (state educational agencies) to understand the data and seek the answers. MCER provides just that: focus and expertise. It's an excellent way to develop the research and collaborative side of the SLDS in tandem with the system as a whole, all the while gaining valuable insight into the state's educational data and policy initiatives. "We're learning a lot from each other," Howell says. "There's a lot of give-and-take among partners in this group."

CONCLUSION

The Career and College Ready Initiative has given Michigan the opportunity to prove the value of its longitudinal data early in the process. Currently, Michigan is about halfway through the MCER project and is gaining key insights into the strengths and limitations of the MMC. Naysayers to the MMC change are starting to see that the sky has not fallen and, according to Howell, "we couldn't have understood what we now do about the MMC without longitudinal data." The project is reinforcing academic changes within the state as well as the SLDS's value and worth. Michigan is developing an SLDS that will provide the data to support the state's drive to produce students who are prepared to thrive in a knowledge economy.

NOTES

Interviews in this chapter conducted by the author with Tom Howell, director of Michigan's Center for Educational Performance and Information (CEPI), SLDS manager, May 31, 2012.

1. CNN, "Detroit Loses a Staggering 25% of Its Population in a Decade," http://articles .cnn.com/2011-03-22/us/michigan.detroit.population_1_census-figures-mayor-dave-bing-undercounting?_s=PM:US (accessed August 2, 2012).

2. NCES, Statewide Longitudinal Data Systems Grant Program: Grantee Information: Michigan, http://nces.ed.gov/programs/slds/state.asp?stateabbr=MI (accessed June 8, 2012).

3. Michigan Merit Curriculum High School Graduation Requirements, Michigan State Board of Education, November 2006, http://www.michigan.gov/documents/ mde/111706-finalhsfaq_178578_7.pdf.

CHAPTER **7**

North Carolina Case Study: New SLDS, Existing Partnerships

The connection between education and workforce has always been acute in North Carolina. North Carolina is the tenth largest state in the nation by population, and it continues to grow. This growth offers many benefits to the state's economy; however, it places strain on the state's educational system. The state sees the connection between its educational system and its economic future: A strong educational system provides a strong knowledge workforce for the years to come. In the latest round of NCES SLDS grants, North Carolina received $3 million to link its K–12 data to higher education and workforce data to further this link between education and whatever comes next for students, with the intention of using it as a more effective gauge of what's working and what's not in education. Though the grant is welcome and appreciated, it's a drop in the bucket beside the $18 million grant the state applied for in the previous round of SLDS grants. North Carolina is a Race to the Top state, though none of the $400 million over four years it is receiving through that program is to be spent on this initiative. Pulling together an SLDS on a shoestring budget with a large group of stakeholders will be a challenge, but one that is a necessary evil if this resource is to be established.

North Carolina is unique in that it has very strong institutions with good working relationships that haven't been able to seal the deal on a strong SLDS as yet. The grant brought together a large group of stakeholders, and the P20W Initiative (as they're calling the grant implementation activities) plans to establish an SLDS for North Carolina. And it's clear that the buy-in among more than just the educational sector is there. North Carolina, though it is approaching formalizing its SLDS later than some states, has very real working relationships across sectors. The exchange of data, although manual and labor intensive, produces reports that other states see as exemplary and are building into their SLDS (including a Community College Feedback Report and a High School Feedback Report). North Carolina also has a cooperative agreement between the Department of Commerce and the state's educational entities that produces longitudinal data reports: the Common Follow-Up System.

North Carolina has tremendous potential to lead the country over the coming years in the area of higher education and workforce connections. As Karl Pond, the P20W team leader and leader of the Data Management Group, which oversees the SLDS within the NCDPI, said wryly as the kickoff meeting began, "Now the fun starts."

STAKEHOLDERS AND THE NC P20W SYSTEM

The North Carolina PK–13 public educational system is run by the North Carolina Department of Public Instruction (NCDPI). The state's SEA currently tracks a large volume of student data using a unique identifier, over 115 school districts (LEAs) and nearly 100 charter schools. NCDPI's Data Management Group (led by Pond) oversees and administers the NCES grant and the P20W Initiative meetings. The P20W Initiative will involve coordinating data with the Department of Commerce, Labor and Economic Analysis Division (DOC-LEAD) and the state's Institutes for Higher Education: the North Carolina Community Colleges System (NCCCS), NC Independent Colleges and Universities (NCICU), and the University of North Carolina system (UNC). NCCCS runs a very successful and effective community college program in the state. Annually, NCCCS's 58 institutions enroll more than three-quarters of a million students on campuses that are within 30 miles of 100 percent of the state's population. The UNC system consists of 17 constituent institutions dedicated to education and research. North Carolina is proud of its public university system, with UNC being the first public university in the United States, chartered in 1789, and the only one to graduate students in the eighteenth century. Today, it continues to offer heavily state-subsidized tuition and top-tier education.

NCICU is comprised of NC's 36 private, nonprofit liberal arts, comprehensive, and research colleges and universities accredited by the Southern Association of Colleges and Schools. NCICU comes to the SLDS project with no existing dataset of its constituent universities; one is being constructed in tandem with the statewide P20W efforts.

The DOC-LEAD is a stakeholder agency that maintains the majority of the workforce data. The DOC-LEAD has a long-standing history of collaboration with North Carolina's education partners. Collaborative efforts have included economic-, workforce- and education-related initiatives.

Two additional state agencies are included as parties to the grant and members of the Governance Board, though not full stakeholders. The North Carolina Division of Motor Vehicles (NCDMV) will provide a key bridge to enable wage data to be matched to student data (through a connection with NCDPI). Through a program connecting student attendance data to drivers' license data (North Carolina suspends the license of a delinquent child under 18), this bridge will be built upon this existing link.

The Early Childhood sector is also at the table, even though the NCES grant is to be spent facilitating the link between PK–13, institutes of higher education and workforce exclusively. Under the RTTT Early Childhood Challenge Grant (ECCG) that NC receives, longitudinal data for the early childhood (EC) sector are a major focus. While the EC sector cannot use funds from the NCES grant on their system, their data are a vital part of the P20W Initiative and they're thus included as stakeholders. Navigating the restrictions of the NCES grant and the RTTT-ECCG terms is challenging in regard to EC data, though communication is enabling the systems to be compatible and designed in tandem. EC is building a similar hub-and-spoke system, using the same UID (unique identifier) process as the P20W system will. "Their hub will be a spoke to our hub," Pond says. Joking aside, this sort of communication and tandem development is important so that the end result is two interoperable datasets.

North Carolina's data system will be set up as a federated data architecture to allow for interagency data sharing and hosted by the NCDPI. The system will require that each agency maintain its own data source files while adhering to data quality procedures and standards (CEDS). Although the final process has yet to be determined, the governing body is working toward developing a process that will evolve as demand increases while keeping true to the various laws and regulations of each sector and the privacy of individual data. Each system will have authorized users who can access the system, with the assumption that researchers already associated with a stakeholder institution will continue to channel data requests through that institution. If it is a new request or more complex, they will turn to the sponsor sector. In the first phase, access won't be given to teachers or administrators, though that's not out of the question for the future.

North Carolina's plan is ambitious and stands to position it as a leader among states in coalition building and teamwork. With a diverse and vested group at the table, North Carolina's P20W stakeholders have high hopes. Some states have been operating an SLDS for 10 years, and North Carolina's entry to the field at this time is being used as an advantage. The technology that exists today makes starting down this path substantially easier. The state is also afforded the added benefit of knowing what sorts of technologies work best for this group of stakeholders, and the ability to cherry-pick the functionality from other states and systems that work well offers some advantages to setting up an SLDS now. Being able to benefit from lessons learned from more established systems is an option that is helpful to all new systems that choose to take advantage; North Carolina is making sure to learn about its predecessors and the technological landscape before making key decisions.

Running Start: A History of Collaboration

In the previous round of NCES SLDS grants in 2009, North Carolina was not chosen. The process alone of proposing the grant in 2009, however, proved to be valuable in strengthening collaborative relationships that have existed since the early 1990s, and mapping the necessary data-sharing protocols. The work on the 2009 grant was parlayed into a valuable beginning for the 2012 grant. North Carolina also implemented a longitudinal database for K–12 data (CEDARS) that enabled it to maintain the framework that, though unfunded initially, is coming into play in the P20W Initiative. A Governance structure exists, the agencies aren't unaccustomed to working together at the start of the grant's funding, and there are many partner agencies invested in the project and its outcomes. North Carolina is beginning this endeavor at an opportune time in its collaborative timeline.

North Carolina has a heritage of using longitudinal data in the Common Follow-Up System (CFS), a cooperative venture authorized by the North Carolina legislature in 1992, directing each of the education sectors to work with the workforce sector to provide an annual report on educational and employment outcomes of students in North Carolina. CFS, incidentally, involves many of the P20W stakeholders. The results of this report are used for "planning, policy making, program evaluation, resource allocation and career planning."[2] It is a valued resource within the state for quality longitudinal data and will continue to run alongside the state's SLDS in the future. The CFS provides longitudinal data for specific domains, and establishes the data-sharing protocol. Though these efforts are fruitful and their results valued, it is clear that a more real-time and ongoing solution would meet the state's rising demands. Additionally, the NCCCS and UNC provide feedback to high schools regarding the performance of their graduates in college (via the High School Feedback Report and Freshman Performance Report). UNC provides similar feedback to the NCCCS regarding its students who later attend North Carolina universities. The Institutes of Higher Education Feedback Report established a loop between teacher preparation programs and their graduates two years postgraduation, an important way that these programs can evaluate their effectiveness and adapt to changes in the education system.

Beyond the regular reports, there are standing agreements to share data among entities as needed, which is largely done using Sneaker Net. For instance, says Pond, "If UNC needed our data, they'd call us up and we'd send it over. If we needed their data, same thing." This process started out with the stakeholders sharing data using a diskette, then CD, then DVD and now a secure ftp download. Even at its most technologically advanced, this is a very manual process for all the parties. "It met the needs at the time," Pond notes. UNC's associate CIO, Steven Hopper, also sees a general agreement in purpose among sectors when it comes to data sharing. However, "it's never easy," he says. This automation, the ability to make the sharing easier and more seamless, is a big selling point of the SLDS grant for the stakeholders.

So, though the SLDS is now supported by the NCES, in many ways North Carolina is able to take a running start, as they've been working together in similar ways over the past few years. The framework is there; now it's time for the data. "We're not sitting at the table trying to figure out what the baseline reports are—we already know that. We're coming to the table knowing what we want," says Pond. "If you think about it, we've been doing this for 15 or 20 years," Pond adds, considering North Carolina's collaborative history and its new technological upgrades. Though the sharing of data and implementing an SLDS were not the precise topics, their working relationships offer a huge potential for success in this project.

Dr. Saundra Williams, Senior Vice President and Chief of Technology and Workforce Development at NCCCS, agrees that the collaborative history among North Carolina's educational entities is a benefit to its SLDS efforts. "Things that may have been issues in other states, for example, governance, are not issues here," she says. The issues the groups have faced in working together have been related to money, she says, in that they didn't receive SLDS grant funding until this year, but it's "never been that one entity wants to share and one doesn't." Between the collaborative history among the agencies and the state-level legislation codifying the governance structure, this piece of North Carolina's SLDS is comparatively simple.

The downside to having such a lengthy and established history of sharing information is that to set up an SLDS will inevitably involve reformulating existing processes. It has worked before, though it wasn't as efficient as it could have been. The process of establishing an SLDS will necessitate memoranda of understanding (MOUs) and legal approvals and some redoing of things that have already been done for years. The ultimate result of this reworking will almost certainly be a better and more robust system, though in the early stages the redundancies are frustrating.

One of the first steps for any SLDS is to obtain signed MOUs from each stakeholder agency to establish the terms of the data sharing and privacy, and ensure everyone "agrees to play nice," says Pond. He admits that this feels a little weird, since he trusts each of the agencies involved and they have such a long history of working together. However, because of the federal money involved, this goodwill is not enough.

THE VISION

With its collaborative history and several grant attempts, there is an underlying motivation in North Carolina's efforts to establish an SLDS. "There is a genuine desire for the sectors to understand what is happening, holistically. Everybody involved understands you need datasets from a variety of areas to fully understand what's going on," says UNC's Steven Hopper. Needing the data to better execute reform and evaluate programs is essential, as is consensus among stakeholders, he says. "In order to help ensure policy changes are going to improve outcomes and have the intended results, one needs integrated data across all sectors," explains Hopper. The P20W project is "essentially creating a framework so everyone can share the data in a seamless way," he adds.

The ability to be more sophisticated in judgments about what's working in the state appeals to Pond and NCDPI as well. Being able to compare two schools that serve the same socioeconomic demographics, even if they're geographically disparate, gives a much more accurate picture than comparing two schools that might be side by side but are comprised of different populations. Pond is intrigued by the potential to make these comparisons more effectively to see what works for different schools. An SLDS, Pond says, gives you the ability to "match like to like in a district, and ultimately like to like across the state and even the country." The longitudinal data also would provide more and better data for judging lower-level programs—like gifted programs, special needs programs or child nutrition programs—and seeing whether they're producing the results they should be.

Dr. Williams sees the system as a tool to "help improve and enhance all sectors of education, including preschool, K–12, community colleges, and universities." Williams is hopeful that the information provided through the system will enable better outcomes in terms of teacher effectiveness, student success, job preparedness and so on. Williams also sees a strong workforce component as a guiding light for the system. "Being able to know how we can help the people of North Carolina move into the workforce successfully, and being able to use the data to track people from school to workforce" is a major benefit of the system, both to the educational sector and to the economy itself, she says. Like many in North Carolina, she sees the education component and workforce component as interconnected and integrated.

STATE LEGISLATION REINFORCING SLDS

When the news was announced that North Carolina had been awarded $3 million to fund its SLDS initiative, the North Carolina General Assembly (NCGA) established further oversight to ensure that the funds and the efforts were being maximized and stayed on track. It established an 18-member board to meet regularly and evaluate the project. Representatives from the stakeholder agencies (as proposed in the grant) were defined as the Governance body, and the legislation added representatives from the General Assembly, the Governor's office and the Superintendent's office for increased oversight.[1] It also codifies many of the terms of the grant, including policies on data sharing, governance and responsibility. It further mandates that the NCDPI provide a quarterly progress report to the NCGA, providing "an update on the implementation of the System's activities, any proposed or planned expansion of System data, and any other recommendations made by the Board, including the most effective and efficient configuration for the System."[3]

This law makes clear that the state of North Carolina is taking this effort seriously, noting the vested interest of these parties in the federal funds. Imposing more regulation and reporting responsibility on a budding system is certainly an added challenge; in early meetings much time was spent trying to parse what exactly the law demanded. Adding more stakeholders and compliance measures adds work, increasing the amount of time needed and hours spent *not* implementing the system. "Governance policy, even in the absence of state law, is hard in and of itself. Trying to make those two work together is harder and politically more challenging," UNC's Hopper observes.

But beyond the added burden, there are some benefits to be realized by working with the NCGA. It provides the opportunity for the North Carolina SLDS effort to have a higher profile among legislators. As members of the working group, their investment in the project should be high and lead to potential state-level funding in the future. This setup, though it is posing additional restrictions and legwork in the beginning, is a maneuver to keep the project from being something that is associated with a political party and brushed aside if (or when) powers shift.

Looking Ahead

Though North Carolina is still in the very early stages of its SLDS, and having access to robust longitudinal data is not yet a reality, stakeholders are enthusiastic about what this access will mean for them. For Dr. Williams, with NCCCS, the SLDS will help with forecasting enrollment, helping NCCCS to better predict "what we're getting from public schools and university systems." With high school students and university students being the two primary sources for North Carolina's community colleges, having more sophisticated predictive modeling for how many students might enroll in a given year would aid in better resource allocation, staffing, and program offerings. "If I'm at a local community college, and I have *x* kids coming in that year, I want to know how to predict how many will move on to local university, how many will enter the workforce, and so on," says Williams. Though the institutions are already "pretty frugal" due to ever-diminishing budgets, Williams notes that this information could help them use their resources in smarter ways.

Further, Williams sees the SLDS as a way to truly gauge the outcomes of their students. Since community college students will often transfer to a four-year institution, or workforce, knowing what became of them is vital to knowing how effective their programs are. Currently, NCCCS's means of tracking former students and graduates into the workforce is spotty (it is dependent upon the students volunteering their Social Security number, which not all students do), and an SLDS would provide more accurate and voluminous data.

Finally, Williams notes that with the data the SLDS will assemble, they hope to better evaluate the effectiveness of their individual institutions. This will enable "decisions to be made based on data, not only statewide, but comparing colleges locally," learning which institutions are succeeding in terms of percentage of graduates obtaining jobs and which are not.

Hopper sees substantial benefit to the UNC system in the automation of data sharing, in which less time will be wasted working out data-sharing procedures inefficiently. He also sees an opportunity for faculty members and researchers who use these data to have access to "more and better grants," doing research on better data and producing more accurate and relevant findings that can ultimately steer state policy. The SLDS is a way for UNC, as well as the other stakeholders, to "not only more efficiently do what we're doing now, but also do more," says Hopper.

CONCLUSION

The SLDS certainly poses a lot of possibilities for increased data use and more efficient service delivery among North Carolina's stakeholder institutions. Both of those benefits, of course, are indelibly connected to the goal of improving student outcomes and the educational system as a whole, and the economy and workforce of North Carolina.

NOTES

Interviews in this chapter conducted by the author with: Karl Pond, enterprise data manager, North Carolina Department of Public Instruction, P20W Project team lead, August 17, 2012; Dr. Saundra Williams, Senior Vice President and Chief of Technology and Workforce Development at NCCCS, September 7, 2012; and Steven Hopper, Associate Chief Information Officer, Application Development & Online Services, University of North Carolina, General Administration, October 19, 2012.

1. Labor & Economic Analysis Division, "A Report on the Operations Of the North Carolina Common Follow-Up System (CFS)," May 2013, http://www.nccommerce.com/Portals/47/Publications/CFS%20Operation%20Report%20May%202013%20Revised.pdf.

2. General Assembly of North Carolina Session 2011, Session Law 2012-133, House Bill 964, http://www.ncga.state.nc.us/Sessions/2011/Bills/House/PDF/H964v5.pdf; General Assembly of North Carolina, Session 2013, House DRH10184-TC-6A, December 2003, http://www.ncleg.net/Applications/BillLookUp/LoadBillDocument.aspx?Session Code=2013&DocNum=3165&SeqNum=0.

3. General Assembly of North Carolina Session 2013, Session Law 2031-80, House Bill 591.

CHAPTER 8

Sharing Information with Others

A ccess to and use of longitudinal data can usher in a new era of accountability for state educational systems, leading to better outcomes for students. In the next two chapters, we focus on how and why the information in the SLDS (statewide longitudinal data system) can and should be shared with those audiences with a right to access it and linking longitudinal data to such systems as the Instructional Improvement System (IIS). The IIS and other transactional systems that help teachers and students in the classroom can benefit from longitudinal data being joined with current assessments and gradebooks to help teachers build an improvement plan for each student based on best practices over many years that can be found in the SLDS. Longitudinal and historical data can be used to improve classroom practice of today and the future. Teachers and administrators have an obvious and ongoing need to access student data, and at a different level than other publics; these groups are discussed in detail in the next chapter. This chapter will outline the other key stakeholder groups as shown in Figure 8.1 that are entitled to access some longitudinal data, and how facilitating that access can make the education system as a whole more successful. For the purposes of Chapters 8 and 9, we will use

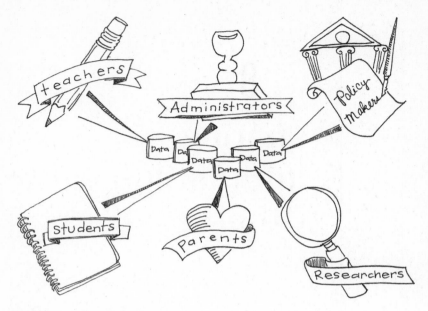

Figure 8.1 SLDS Stakeholders

longitudinal data to describe the output from the SLDS, a set of reports used to help make better decisions in these other systems.

Longitudinal data are a resource for the state and are comprised of the outcomes of many years of graduating classes. These data, when properly used, can inform how we respond when intervention is needed for a particular student. Like the amazon.com recommendation engine, longitudinal data can help the current student based on what worked in the past.

A major part of the dissemination of longitudinal data will involve mapping out who will be given access to the data, and what data they should be authorized to see. A key purpose of an SLDS is to share information with entitled parties, not to keep it locked up, and a key exercise in its establishment will be making the data accessible to different groups of users. It should be thought of as a public project with stakeholders ranging from teachers and administrators to parents, students, the public, policy makers and researchers, groups that might not currently have ready access to as much data as they should. These secondary groups are entitled to access *certain* data contained in the SLDS, and it now becomes the job of the SLDS to make systems to support sharing these data to these groups. Wider access to educational data is a key deliverable for any SLDS project, and one that states are largely lagging in.[1]

Different groups of stakeholders are legally entitled to different information and the educational system has an obligation to share that information. Legally, states can't share protected student information (such as personally identifiable information, discussed in Chapter 3) with the general public, though students and their parents are entitled to this information. There are many nuances to sharing information with the public and with various stakeholder groups; however, there are many benefits of sharing the right information with the right group. It's a major opportunity for those who operate the educational system (educators and administrators) and also for those who have children in it, fund it through tax dollars and vote on its leaders. FERPA (Family Educational Rights and Privacy Act) sets stringent restrictions for protecting student information and governs who should have access to certain data an SLDS contains. Additionally, FERPA and some state laws further mandate that the educational system provide access to certain user groups, a measure that an SLDS will make more streamlined. It's a complex regulation, and one that was developed (and amended) with the students' interests in mind. In using longitudinal data, the goal is to protect the student while being accountable to the public and providing information to which they're entitled access. To fully maximize the investment in the SLDS and provide information to stakeholders who aren't employees of the educational system, navigating this balance is essential.

If the system is set up using access groups (as it should be), this sort of limited access is not difficult to implement. Each user group will need and be eligible for access to certain information, depending on their role, and be prohibited from seeing other personally identifiable information. For example, administrators and teachers need to be able to access student records for the students in their class or school, including private data. Parents are entitled to see their child's student record, but not those of other students.

PUBLIC INFORMATION SHARING: WHAT INFORMATION IS THE PUBLIC ENTITLED TO AND INTERESTED IN?

There are many reasons the general public might be interested in data about their schools. The school system is obligated to provide these data, and the SLDS offers an automated way to provide that access. The DQC also stresses that the general public and parent stakeholders seeking information on school performance are entitled to aggregate statistics that use longitudinal data, protecting individually identifiable student and teacher information.[2] Parents have an obvious stake in seeing these data in making educational decisions for their children, but the general public also has a right to see how their tax dollars are being spent and judge whether their educational leaders are succeeding at delivering a good education.[3] The public's primary motivations for accessing education data are to *inform decisions* and *see outcome-related reports* to judge the effectiveness of their leaders and initiatives.

There are two ways to meet these objectives. The first entails sharing longitudinal data through a set of standard reports of important outcome-based information, such as a high school performance report that shares statistics on how students fare after high school. Another way to share relevant data with the public to inform their decisions is to make available analyzed and searchable information for users to peruse. These sets of reports are selected based on the number of requests and popular demand.

Data on the value-added score for each of the 11,500 teachers in the Los Angeles Unified School District were recently made publicly available by the *Los Angeles Times* in the form of a teacher ranking, a hotly contested form of sharing school and teacher performance data with the public. The *Times* took the publicly available value-added teacher data (requested under the California Public Records Act from the LA Unified School District), aggregated it, analyzed it and included other factors to rank teachers by effectiveness. The *Times* has published these data in a searchable database for all LA teachers of grades 3–5. The *Times* argues that "teachers are the single most important school-related factor in a child's education" and parents are entitled to objective information on the effectiveness of their child's teacher.[4] This sort of resource can be a boon for parents looking to make data-driven educational decisions.

Additionally, an SLDS can provide aggregated data to the public in the form of feedback reports, while protecting student privacy. A high school feedback report will shed light on the weaknesses or strengths of a high school, providing aggregated information on students' post-secondary enrollment, success (such as remediation or degree completion) and even employment.[5] This information is important in assessing whether schools are effectively preparing students to succeed in college and careers, and communicating this information to the public offers high levels of transparency to ensure schools are held accountable.

POLICY MAKERS AND STATE-LEVEL DECISION MAKERS: HOW CAN LEGISLATORS ENABLE AND USE LONGITUDINAL DATA?

Policy makers' role in SLDSs is two pronged: enablers and users. They have the ability to enable the sharing of appropriate information to entitled stakeholders, by ensuring that state laws aren't overly restrictive and are within the FERPA limitations, and they are also users of the data in the SLDS. Longitudinal data will allow them to make more informed policy decisions and better evaluate educational initiatives. We see it as a best practice for SLDS committees to work with policy makers and state-level decision makers closely. Legislators need to understand the need for longitudinal data and the nuances of working with them.[6] Working with policy makers also ensures a mutually beneficial legal atmosphere for the SLDS, as well as bipartisan support for the project and executive buy-in. Even with several years of federal grant funding, the SLDS will eventually need to be sustained on its own; making state-level connections provides the opportunity for future support.

Enabling Longitudinal Data Use: Setting Policy Surrounding the SLDS

The policy makers (local, state and federal legislators) are the gatekeepers to the SLDS for various publics. Laws governing the sharing of student and educational data vary by state and can prevent wide access to longitudinal data, even as allowed by FERPA. FERPA effectively sets the bar nationally on student ownership of their educational records and privacy standards; however, individual states can make their own laws further restricting the information. "State law can be more restrictive than FERPA, but it can't be less restrictive than FERPA," according to Baron Rodriguez, director of the Privacy Technical Assistance Center (PTAC) (a division of the U.S. Educational Department [USED]).[7] To that end, some states have laws on the books either reiterating FERPA or imposing more stringent laws limiting the sharing and storing of student data. These laws can hamper the interagency sharing of data that an SLDS might need. In these cases, a policy maker amending existing legislation to allow for this type of system is essential to forward movement. Beyond removing legal restrictions that could prohibit the establishment and functioning of an SLDS, state-level policy makers can create legislation to maintain the SLDS, ensuring that parties to the system share the correct information with one another and the entitled publics while staying within FERPA's restrictions.

Policy makers can provide funding to safeguard the SLDS's future, ensuring that the system won't be a political project of one party and thwarted if political power shifts. Policies and authorization criteria set out by Governance can be established as law by policy makers, better communicating these resources to the public and stakeholders and ensuring their future access. It is also incumbent on policy makers to portray longitudinal data in accurate and responsible ways, helping to educate the public about what is shared and protected and why it is essential. All of these things can make the SLDS more accessible and popular among the general population, and more useful to the target audiences. Though it creates added layers of compliance, it ensures stakeholders are legally bound to the SLDS and data sharing.

Users of Longitudinal Data

Policy makers are also users of longitudinal data. At the state level, governors, chief state school officers and legislators can all make use of longitudinal data to better evaluate programs, learn about the state's student population trends and make smarter funding allocations.[8] In the examples we offered in Chapter 1, the legislature's desire to evaluate the Instructional Improvement System as well as the governor's desire to impact the state's dropout rate through an early warning system are both examples of policy makers depending on longitudinal data to drive their decisions. These data provide the opportunity for rich analysis and information, with the ability to better evaluate whether reforms are effective and spot trends as they're emerging. Rather than data cobbled together from various sources, or data that are several years old, real-time, accurate and longitudinal data can be used to drive state-level policy. This means better allocation of resources, and ultimately, a better education for students. "Without access to timely and accurate data, state policy makers are flying blind when weighing the potential impact of new legislation in terms of the cost, return on investment, and effect on students and schools."[9] Policy makers need access to longitudinal data to avoid making policy judgments based on intuition. Policy makers' access to longitudinal data will likely be on an ad hoc basis; when a question comes up or law needs support, they can requisition the state's educational authority or an affiliated research group to perform the necessary reporting and analysis.

Program Assessment

The best way to ensure the value and continued relevance of the SLDS is to prove that it is useful to policy makers, involving them in each stage of the process to promote interest, and ensuring that the system provides them with timely, accurate and needed data. In short, by functioning properly, the SLDS can demonstrate its worth to the stakeholders who have the most power to advocate for its continued funding and use. To retain policy maker support and enthusiasm, the system needs to be able to answer questions policy makers pose. Having policy makers in mind when the system is designed and addressing their needs along the way is important to the sustainability of the system. Therefore, it is important that the system is built with policy maker input and with respect to their anticipated usage of the system. As both enablers and users of the SLDS, policy makers are important stakeholders to consider throughout the process.

RESEARCHERS: HOW CAN STATES LEVERAGE RESEARCHERS TO MAKE THE LONGITUDINAL DATA ANSWER KEY QUESTIONS?

With SLDSs, states are assembling an unprecedented amount of data, with the potential to tell us so much about the educational system as a whole: what reforms and programs are working, detecting trends before they might be obvious and allowing for earlier intervention, and identifying gaps and overlaps in the system. However, those answers don't just materialize out of a data system; research and analysis must be done to ask the right questions, survey the right data and analyze it. Providing data to individuals with high-level analytical training and research skills for analysis, mining and surveying is an important way for states to make full use of the longitudinal data they're collecting.[10] This partnership between the SEA (state educational agencies) and researchers, as well as a solid research agenda, is a way to accomplish the high-level analytical functions that can provide information to drive decisions. So much time and effort is spent in establishing the SLDS, the use and analysis of the data to improve the education system might be overlooked.

Research Agenda

How do states go about ensuring the longitudinal data are used? Establishing a research agenda and discussing it early and often in the planning and implementation helps to keep the goal in mind and develop the system around the information being sought. Research universities, data scientists and independent agencies should be included in the development and execution of the research agenda.[11]

Setting a public policy regarding data use and which data are available publicly from the SLDS is a good idea. This establishes early that the intent of the system isn't to collect information and keep it locked up, but to share what can be shared with those interested parties.[12] This sort of policy can also explicitly lay out who will have access to what information. Additionally, collecting memoranda of understanding (MOUs) from researchers further sets rules for data use and sharing and establishes an agreement surrounding data ownership and privacy policy.

Launching a partnership with a research university is one way to foster research activities, such as the relationship that exists between the North Carolina Education Research Data Center (NCERDC) at Duke University and the North Carolina Department of Public Instruction (NCDPI). NCERDC maintains the database of North Carolina students and teachers while making the data available to university and nonprofit policy researchers.[13] Another option to ensure the use of the longitudinal data is to establish educational research centers at the state level. Texas did just this in 2008, working with the Family Policy Compliance Office (FPCO) to stay within FERPA regulations and maintaining student privacy. The state legislature funded three educational research centers that are responsible for accommodating research requests as they come in, providing remote access for researchers, and maintaining student privacy under FERPA.[14]

Providing proper training to researchers to ensure they are able to use the system, read the data with accuracy and are aware of what types of questions the system can handle is a key effort during the implementation and early phases of your state's SLDS. A fear many SEAs have with allowing researcher access to longitudinal data is that researchers might misunderstand certain data fields, leading to incorrect analysis and conclusions. Be proactive in the researchers' understanding; communicate explicitly what is available and how it is to be understood and defined.

Improving Educational Research

Some fields, such as medicine, have decades of progressive, common knowledge, an entire body of research leading to consensus about what outcomes are in certain situations, how peripheral factors affect outcomes and what actions can remedy specific issues. What was once considered unpredictable is now widely understood and accepted. Medical research has moved from addressing symptoms to diagnosing causes and even prevention. Educational research, currently, is not yet this advanced. With increases in the availability and the breadth of educational research, we believe the same development is possible for educational research.

In education, many conflicting, sometimes completely opposite, theories are researched, supported and published, leaving administrators and teachers without a strong body of research pointing them in one direction on a variety of issues. The problem lies in the data available to today's educational researchers. Currently, educational researchers aren't able to obtain the necessary data and depth of data to ascertain causality, and correlation (a much less certain relationship) is the most they can make a case for. This uncertain correlating research is often such that several answers to the same question could be acceptable, leading to the great contention and uncertainty among practitioners.[15]

How can educational research create consensus and establish causal relationships? Longitudinal data provide an unprecedented opportunity for researchers to have access to timely and rich datasets and produce reliable results. Similar to how medical research evolved from trying to understand symptoms to research on causes, educational research, too, can move from making generalizations for all students (by age, race, gender, etc.) and move toward a greater understanding for each individual student. With more and better data, more differentiating factors can set each student apart, including a variety of factors and circumstances in the discussion.

Truly, the possibilities discussed in this book hinge on a maturing field of educational research, one that seeks to make causal connections supported by longitudinal data and promote better student outcomes. Only with wide researcher access to longitudinal data can this body of research be established and consensus built around what is best for the educational system.

To maximize the usefulness of the longitudinal data, states should facilitate research partnerships and promote an agreed-upon research agenda that seeks to gain an understanding of the state's educational system and efforts. Having solid evidence on what is working and what is failing in regard to special programs, policies, reform initiatives, curricula, and teaching practices is an exciting prospect for anyone with a stake in our educational system.

ESTABLISHING THE CONNECTION WITH ACADEMIA

For SLDSs, the connection to academia and research universities is a natural one; many systems are collecting data from these institutions to begin with. The state department of education wants to ask deep questions, evaluating its initiatives and making sure it is funding the appropriate things, but often lacks the expertise, time and objectivity to effectively do this. Researchers need access to rich datasets. Partnering with academic researchers offers a convenient and mutually beneficial opportunity to use more complete datasets and derive more reliable results, satisfying the needs of the state. Having researchers use and access the data regularly for research also affords the state another opportunity for accountability and data quality control. Allowing approved institutes of research to access and analyze a state's longitudinal data is a win-win scenario.

Broadly, it's vital to have a plan for who is going to research using the longitudinal data. One option is to make connections with research universities that are able to analyze the data in the SLDS and work with the state's research agenda, focusing on issues and statistics that impact the SEA's operations. SEAs and researchers can establish the key questions together. Rich longitudinal data are an excellent resource for researchers; however, it's equally important to continually reinforce and remind researchers what data are there and how to access them.

Data Scientists

With the rise of big data across industries, a need to make connections and inferences about data and trends has developed. The field of *data science* has emerged to provide these crucial skills and tools to turn data into usable information. *Data scientists* deal with *big data*, the widely accepted term for "large, diverse, complex, longitudinal, and/or distributed data sets" coming from various and disparate systems and in differing formats.[16] The National Science Foundation (NSF) sees the big data issue in broad terms, across industries and professions. "Today, scientists, biomedical researchers, engineers, educators, citizens and decision-makers live in an era of observation: Data come from many disparate sources, such as sensor networks; scientific instruments, such as medical equipment, telescopes, colliders, satellites, environmental networks, and scanners; video, audio, and click streams; financial transaction data; email, weblogs, Twitter feeds, and picture archives; spatial graphs and maps; and scientific simulations and models."[17] SLDSs certainly fit in the big data box, with many sources of data and many types of data. How do states navigate the nuances and differences in their data, making sure that little differences don't mean the data are ignored or unused? For states embarking on the SLDS creation or improvement journey, a data scientist could be a valuable addition to the SLDS effort. Someone to make sense of the data and make connections intelligently will increase the overall value of the system.

For systems dealing with an unprecedented amount of data, like educational SLDSs, a data scientist could be a key player. "More than anything, what data scientists do is make discoveries while swimming in data."[18] They're responsible for making discoveries (finding patterns and trends), communicating these findings in intelligible ways to stakeholders who might not be as data-savvy, all utilizing a highly technical background with training in code-writing and science.[19] It's a highly specialized job description, requiring the curiosity and intellect of a scientist with the skills of a computer scientist, and communication—both verbal and visual—abilities to boot. A good data scientist will do more than simply address a given problem; he or she can choose the right problem.[20]

This newfound niche within the world of big data, and across many industries and sectors, is coming up a bit empty; there is a gap between qualified professionals and demand in the field. The NSF recently started a program called the Core Techniques and Technologies for Advancing Big Data Science and Engineering, also referred to as BIGDATA. This initiative aims to accelerate the speed of field research and development of professional skills and tools and stimulate interest in big data.[21] Recognizing, broadly, that being able to fully utilize the vast amounts of longitudinal data we currently hold to make better data-driven decisions with the goal of enabling "breakthrough discoveries and innovation in science, engineering, medicine, commerce, education, and national security, laying the foundations for U.S. competitiveness for many decades to come," the NSF is encouraging and funding projects focused on furthering this field, hoping to foster the next generation of data scientists.[22]

Sean Mulvenon of the University of Arkansas advocates for researchers who fully understand the issues at stake and the datasets, saying that the researcher is not simply the "problem finder," but the *framer* of the issues. He says, "What's important about [the way researchers approach problems] is we have to do it in a positive, proactive way. Just saying 'this program didn't work' is not enough, and it's a fundamental mistake from researchers." While it isn't incumbent on researchers to solve all issues, Mulvenon challenges them to do more than simply point out shortcomings in state educational systems if they seek to prove their worth and retain high regard.[23]

In the past, this sort of whistleblowing research that has simply alerted the state (and sometimes the public) to a problem has earned educational researchers some disdain from those who hold the data. Sadly, this can result in less willingness to share, under the assumption that the researchers are only out to expose shortcomings and make the state look bad, or that the researchers might misinterpret the data and make incorrect assumptions. We hold that greater training and communication can help build trust with the research community. An involved and active research community is very important to the SLDS, as the expertise and skills researchers bring are unparalleled by any other user group. Indeed, the mutual benefit from working closely with research institutions is not to be understated. Schools have ready access to trained analysts, statisticians and subject-matter experts with a keen interest in longitudinal data. Their interests can make new, objective connections and serve to advance the educational system.

Establishing Protocols for Data Access

The National Forum on Education Statistics notes that "responding to data requests is a substantial undertaking that must be managed effectively given its demand on SEA resources and far-reaching implications on the quality of educational research."[24] Without an automated and structured system, it can be time consuming and tedious for SEA employees to gather data as requested by researchers. It is therefore important for SEAs to have established evaluation criteria upon which to decide who should have access and how that access will be granted. Proper planning, strong policies and good communication with researchers can help the process be less cumbersome and still beneficial. Before SEAs begin sharing data with researchers, it's vital to establish who should be authorized to receive data from the SLDS, a fair timeline for the researcher to receive, analyze and surrender the data, fees that will be charged to the requester (if any), and restrictions on data security and destruction.[25] The more organized and automated the system is, the less of a burden it will be on the SEAs, enabling them to reap the benefits from having expert research performed on their longitudinal data. Establishing these protocols will be part of Governance's responsibilities.

First, a best practice is to publish as much nonsensitive (cell-suppressed) data on the Web as possible. The more that is readily available on the Internet, the less legwork the SEA will have to do to fulfill researcher requests for this basic information. Next, it's important to clearly communicate what is provided to head off requests for information that is publicly available. Including tutorials or online documentation about what information is available publicly (without submitting a request) and what information is available upon request is a best practice. For example, the Kansas State Department of Education offers videos with a quiz afterward to ensure that researchers aren't bypassing the information that is provided. Requesters must certify that they've reviewed the data that are currently available as well.[26] There should be a data request form (submitted electronically, most likely) and a consistent way to evaluate each proposal. If the proposal is denied, it's a best practice to communicate to the researcher what changes might lead to acceptance.[27]

FERPA requires that SEAs keep track of all releases of data to researchers.[28] It is incumbent on the SEAs to track the information that was released until a data destruction certification is received.[29] It is up to the individual agency if there should be a review of the research to sign off on the data use or findings before publication or public release. Generally, SEAs should review the use of the data to ensure they were within the state definitions of data and no incorrect assumptions were made, but shouldn't judge research based on the conclusions (even if they are potentially damaging to the state's reputation).[30]

PARENTS: WHAT LONGITUDINAL DATA DO PARENTS NEED, AND HOW WILL IT MAKE A DIFFERENCE?

One of the shifts in the educational system we discuss in this book (and at length in Chapter 10) is the move from relying solely on academic achievement as a means for gauging success to seeing the learning that occurs outside of the classroom as formative and impactful on student outcomes. With this new way of viewing a child's multifaceted education comes a changed understanding of the role of parents. One of the most powerful factors in a child's education is family engagement.[31]

When we talk about improving student outcomes, parental involvement is a key factor in the discussion. Studies have shown that students with highly involved parents consistently score higher than those with less involved parents.[32] Parental expectation is the factor that has the biggest impact on student achievement, research shows.[33] The systemic shift, in recognizing all of a student's time as impactful, elevates parents to a primary stakeholder role and necessitates greater involvement and communication; including parents in the use of longitudinal data makes it easier for them to fulfill their role in their child's education and improves outcomes on the individual level. With longitudinal data, parents, too, should be able to make data-driven decisions.

Systemic Shift: Parents as Stakeholders in Student Outcomes

As a stakeholder group, parents hold a lot of power over their child's education and outcomes. A systemic shift among educational entities to recognize the increased value and expectation of the parents as major stakeholders in their child's educational outcome is required. SLDSs offer a prime opportunity to provide parents with access to useful student educational data so they can play their role as informed stakeholders. Providing parents with appropriate, up-to-date and actionable information is an excellent way to effect change in student outcomes.

For parents who want to be involved but don't know how, and for parents who are involved but want a better system for receiving updates, access to these data using the SLDS is an ideal solution. However, not all parents are created equal. What about the parents who are less involved in their child's education? While it's never going to be the case that all parents play an active and engaged role in their child's education, access to data about their child and information providing recommended actions and ways to be involved are means to provide more opportunities for less involved parents, and perhaps, encourage a greater number of parents to take an active role. Having these kinds of data and involving the parents more often changes the way that parents are seen in the educational system by all stakeholders. Family engagement becomes automatically enabled and trackable, a part of the normal course of business.[34]

Under FERPA, parents are granted "certain rights with regard to their children's education records, such as the right to inspect and review [their] child's education records."[35] Online access to up-to-date information in any automated way is uncommon. Today, parents are not typically given classroom and achievement data in a timely or ongoing manner, meaning their expectations aren't necessarily based on reality and they're also at a loss on what to do to help their child.[36] This is a major benefit that longitudinal data reports offer: the ability for parents to know what is going on as their child progresses, and how to best help their student.

Parental Data Access

Certain datasets can be very useful without much training or explanation. Parents are already entitled to receive this information today, but old systems require a formal request or indirect access (through the student), making the delivery systems unreliable and sometimes requiring a great deal of effort on the LEA's and the parents' part. Parents might want to access student attendance records, growth in learning data, disciplinary records, credits earned and graduation track status, summative and formative assessment scores, and program enrollment status.[37] This information can help the parents play a more informed, proactive role in things like goal-setting, homework help and even enrichment activities, helping their child reach new levels of mastery.[38] Additionally, aggregated data that show the quality of their child's school can help the parents to make informed educational choices.[39]

As with any other user group, the data that parents receive should be in a format that is contextualized and actionable. Showing a student test score isn't enough. Showing how it relates to peers, to national averages, expectations for that particular student, and at what point he is in danger of failing the grade are useful contextualizing data points. Additionally, giving suggested methods for increasing test scores or challenging a student with consistently high scores are examples of providing the actions to support parental involvement. Positioning the information alongside college and career readiness and grade expectations is another way to contextualize this information for parents.[40] Ultimately, to be useful to parents, the information has to be actionable, giving parents the resources and context necessary to effect change in the outcome if needed.[41]

In-person conversations are great opportunities to reinforce the importance of data and the SLDS in making educational decisions and judgments.[42] Using these opportunities to educate parents on data use and demonstrate how to access and use it is a best practice. Parent–teacher conferences and parent orientation events are great times to discuss and reinforce data access and use.

Goals of Increased Access for Parents

Discussions that are driven by data among teachers, administrators and parents add more depth and meaning to what is being said. With all stakeholders having the same information, something like a parent–teacher conference can begin at a much different place than if the parents are receiving data for the first time at the meeting. Conversations can be ongoing, with less of the onus on the teacher to provide information and potential remedies for the parents. Additionally, once the data are introduced, it changes the expectation for the better. In schools where increased access has been granted to parents, "experience suggests that parents are creating a demand for data that can inform, if not deepen, communication between families and schools." As Bill Tucker of Education Sector points out, parents will no longer be satisfied with "Fine" as a response to the question, "How is my child doing?" Providing ongoing data to the parents creates potential for conversations that are more engaging and results-oriented.[43] In a world where instant information is available on most important things—a parent can instantly find the balance on a credit card or bank account, for instance—expecting this responsiveness for their child's educational records isn't too far-fetched.

Giving parents more access to aggregated information about the schools provides increased overall accountability. If parents are given choice among certain schools in a district, having ongoing access to achievement data makes for more informed decisions by the parents, and holds each school accountable.

And, ultimately, providing parents with increased access and more information can lead to better student outcomes. More informed processes, such as realistic goal setting, directed study and remediating issues quicker, offer tremendous potential in enhancing student outcomes. One of the advantages of longitudinal data that we've noted is creating opportunities for early intervention. Parents could see early warnings that their child is not on track to graduate on time, or that he or she is within the achievement guidelines to qualify for admission to a certain college. Providing early warning alerts to parents, the stakeholders with the most direct access to and impact on the student, is a key advantage.

STUDENTS: HOW CAN SCHOOLS PROVIDE STUDENTS WITH MORE INTUITIVE, INSTANT ACCESS TO THEIR OWN STUDENT RECORD CONTEXTUALIZED WITH LONGITUDINAL DATA?

FERPA's primary purpose is to establish students as the owners of their own educational data, and educators as the stewards of it. Given this policy, it's rather alarming that students have such minimal access to their student records in today's classrooms.

If presented in the right way, data can be "an absolute game-changer," according to Michelle Rhee, at the Data Quality Campaign's Data Summit in early 2012. She noted that in one particular school where students were given access to the data, it led to greater student investment in the outcomes. They were trying to "out-achieve" each other, and kept tabs on the data often. Because of the school's 20 percent growth that year, the students became invested, even "obsessed with the data." Rhee said they checked their status frequently, informally competing with one another. "They are not going to be satisfied with 4 or 5 percent (improvement in the coming year), they have set a much loftier goal for themselves," said Rhee. In this school, the data changed the expectations from the children and made them more demanding consumers, extending those expectations to more engaging lessons and real-time data. In this school, providing the students with data motivated them in an unprecedented way. "If you have the data, and you can invest and engage children and their families in these data, it can change a culture quickly," she noted.[44]

"I think we dramatically underutilize the strategy of empowering kids with their own data," Secretary of Education Arne Duncan said.[45] Instilling a sense of pride and establishing a feedback loop surrounding a student's data are effective and logical ways to gain interest from today's generation of video-gamer kids. "They love the score, they love the feedback," he notes. And what's more, they're accustomed to this nearly instantaneous feedback, and the education experience should be no different. This sort of feedback can provide motivation to achieve, and Duncan notes that "we can become a lot more strategic and systematic in doing that."[46]

Indeed, the Institute of Education Sciences (IES) recommends teaching students to examine and evaluate their own data and use it to form learning goals.[47] This practice serves two purposes. First, it invests students in the educational process, providing motivation to reach a goal and satisfaction upon successfully meeting it. Second, it empowers them as full stakeholders in their own education, giving them control over learning goals and a sense of accomplishment. Truly, in the world after school, students are responsible for their own goal setting and attaining, so this skill is useful and worth learning early. A common outcome from this access is that teachers can learn about what motivates the student through the self-selected goals and adjust their teaching methods accordingly.[48] Indeed, as the above anecdotes point out, data can often motivate students to higher achievement.

Certainly, a school cannot simply give students all of the data. Targeting specific learning-related datasets and educating students on how to contextualize them and make goals based on those datasets is a best practice. It's important to "explain expectations and assessment criteria," noting what is expected, creating individual goals and outlining classroom goals.[49] A great way to communicate how a student will be evaluated is by using a rubric, noting what is necessary to qualify for each rating. Additionally, using a rubric to give grades back provides a feedback mechanism for students to see contextualized results. Though this certainly is not an iconoclastic idea by any means, the theory behind it—involving students in the context and reasoning for their grades—helps set the tone for their involvement in data and learning outcomes.

Another key recommendation from IES is to provide feedback to students in a timely manner, a task made substantially simpler with the implementation of an SLDS.[50] One of the main benefits of such a system is timely access to updated information. When dealing with grades and outcomes, the closer the feedback can be to when the assignment or test occurred, the more valuable it is to the student in terms of relevance.

Providing students with more detailed and immediate access to their academic information, and the context and knowledge to interpret it, essentially elevates them to where they belong: as primary stakeholders in their educational success. Of course, the student is ultimately responsible for his or her success, and providing the data to drive better goal-setting and learning is logical if one hopes for a better result. Facilitating goal-setting and targeted learning provides more directed information for other individualized learning initiatives and gives teachers more data to guide their instruction.

CONCLUSION

It is important to keep these stakeholder groups in consideration as the SLDS is constructed and the processes designed. Providing increased and smarter access to policy makers, researchers, parents and students is a primary purpose of an SLDS, and this access can in turn offer many benefits to the educational system and students. While there are definitely challenges to be overcome in facilitating access to these user groups, the benefits—increased levels of engagement, transparency, and improved student outcomes—are vital to the education system as a whole.

NOTES

1. Data for Action 2012, "Focus on People to Change Data Culture," Data Quality Campaign annual report (November 2012).
2. Data Quality Campaign, "10 State Actions to Ensure Effective Data Use: Implement Systems to Provide Timely Access to Information," http://dataqualitycampaign.org/build/actions/5/ (accessed August 23, 2012).
3. NCES, "Traveling Through Time: The Forum Guide to Longitudinal Data Systems Book 4: Advanced LDS Usage," http://nces.ed.gov/pubsearch/pubsinfo.asp?pubid=2011802.
4. *Los Angeles Times*, "Los Angeles Teacher Ratings FAQ and About," http://projects.latimes.com/value-added/faq/#publish_scores (accessed January 17, 2013).
5. Amilcar Guzman, "High School Feedback DFA2012 Fact Sheet Released Today," January 14, 2013, http://www.dataqualitycampaign.org/2013/01/14/High-School-Feedback-DFA2012-Fact-Sheet-Released-Today (accessed January 17, 2013). http://www.dataqualitycampaign.org/stateanalysis/actions/10.
6. Karl Pond, interview with author, August 1, 2013.
7. Baron Rodriguez, interview with author, June 13, 2012.

8. NCES, "Traveling Through Time."

9. Data Quality Campaign, "10 State Actions to Ensure Effective Data Use: Promote Strategies to Raise Awareness of Available Data," http://www.dataqualitycampaign .org/stateanalysis/actions/10 (accessed September 6, 2012).

10. "Ensuring Effective Data Use in Education," SAS White Paper.

11. Data Quality Campaign, "State Analysis by Action: Develop a P-20/Workforce Research Agenda," http://dataqualitycampaign.org/stateanalysis/actions/8/ (accessed August 22, 2012).

12. Tate Gould, "Why the Research Community Should Take Notice of Statewide Longitudinal Data Systems," Institute of Education Sciences, Fourth Annual IES Research Conference, Concurrent Panel Session, June 9, 2009, http://ies.ed.gov/ director/conferences/09ies_conference/presentations/transcripts/presentation4.pdf (accessed August 23, 2012).

13. Duke University, Center for Child and Family Policy, "Projects: North Carolina Education Research Data Center (NCERDC)," http://www.childandfamilypolicy.duke. edu/project_detail.php?id=35 (accessed August 1, 2013).

14. Dan O'Brien, "The Texas FERPA Story," CALDER Brief, November 2008, http://www .caldercenter.org/UploadedPDF/1001267_texasferpastory.pdf (accessed August 23, 2012).

15. Clayton M. Christensen, Michael B. Horn, and Curtis W. Johnson, *Disrupting Class: How Disruptive Innovation Will Change the Way the World Learns* (New York: McGraw-Hill, 2008).

16. National Science Foundation, "Core Techniques and Technologies for Advancing Big Data Science & Engineering (BIGDATA)," program solicitation, June 13, 2012, http://www.nsf.gov/pubs/2012/nsf12499/nsf12499.pdf.

17. Ibid.

18. Thomas H. Davenport and D. J. Patil, "Data Scientist: The Sexiest Job of the 21st Century," http://hbr.org/2012/10/data-scientist-the-sexiest-job-of-the-21st-century/ar/1 (accessed October 5, 2012).

19. Ibid.

20. IBM, "What Is a Data Scientist?," http://www-01.ibm.com/software/data/infosphere/ data-scientist/ (accessed October 3, 2012).

21. National Science Foundation, "Core Techniques and Technologies for Advancing Big Data Science & Engineering (BIGDATA)."

22. Ibid.

23. Sean Mulvenon, interview with author, April 24, 2012.

24. National Forum on Education Statistics, "Forum Guide to Supporting Data Access for Researchers: A State Education Agency Perspective" (July 2012).

25. Ibid.

26. Kathy Gosa, "Facilitating Researcher Access to State Wide Longitudinal Data Systems," NCES MIS Conference, February 13, 2013.

27. National Forum on Education Statistics, "Forum Guide to Supporting Data Access for Researchers: A State Education Agency Perspective."

28. Kathy Gosa, "Facilitating Researcher Access to State Wide Longitudinal Data Systems."

29. National Forum on Education Statistics, "Forum Guide to Supporting Data Access for Researchers: A State Education Agency Perspective."

30. Bethann Canada, "Facilitating Researcher Access to State Wide Longitudinal Data Systems," NCES MIS Conference, February 13, 2013.

31. Heather B. Weiss, M. Elena Lopez, and Deborah R. Stark, "Breaking New Ground: Data Systems Transform Family Engagement in Education," PTA & Harvard Family Research Project Issue Briefs: Family Engagement Policy and Practice, January 2011, http://www.hfrp.org/publications-resources/browse-our-publications/breaking-new-ground-data-systems-transform-family-engagement-in-education2 (accessed August 21, 2012).

32. William H. Jeynes, "Parental Involvement and Student Achievement: A Meta-Analysis," Family Involvement Research Digests: Harvard Family and Research Project, December 2005, http://www.hfrp.org/publications-resources/browse-our-publications/parental-involvement-and-student-achievement-a-meta-analysis (accessed August 20, 2012).

33. Data Quality Campaign, "Hot Topic: Empowering Parents with Data," 2011, http://www.dataqualitycampaign.org/resources/details/1591 (accessed August 21, 2012).

34. Weiss, Lopez, and Stark, "Breaking New Ground."

35. FERPA, http://www.ed.gov/policy/gen/guid/fpco/ferpa/index.html.

36. Weiss, Lopez, and Stark, "Breaking New Ground."

37. NCES, "Traveling Through Time."

38. Weiss, Lopez, and Stark, "Breaking New Ground."

39. Data Quality Campaign, "Hot Topic."

40. Weiss, Lopez, and Stark, "Breaking New Ground."

41. Ibid.

42. Ibid.

43. Ibid.

44. Michelle Rhee, "DQC's National Data Summit," January 18, 2012, http://dataqualitycampaign.org/events/details/299 (accessed August 21, 2012).

45. Arne Duncan, *DQC's National Data Summit*, January 18, 2012, http://dataqualitycampaign.org/events/details/299 (accessed August 21, 2012).

46. Ibid.

47. L. Hamilton, R. Halverson, S. Jackson, E. Mandinach, J. Supovitz, and J. Wayman, *Using Student Achievement Data to Support Instructional Decision Making (NCEE 2009–4067)* (Washington, DC: National Center for Education Evaluation and Regional Assistance, Institute of Education Sciences, U.S. Department of Education, 2009); retrieved from http://ies.ed.gov/ncee/wwc/publications/practiceguides/.

48. Rhonda Barton, "Fostering a Data-Driven Culture," *Education Northwest* 16, no. 9 (2011): 6–9, http://educationnorthwest.org/webfm_send/1130.

49. Hamilton, Halverson, Jackson, Mandinach, Supovitz, and Wayman, *Using Student Achievement Data to Support Instructional Decision Making (NCEE 2009–4067)*.

50. Ibid.

CHAPTER **9**

Using Data in Schools and Classrooms

Teachers and administrators have perhaps the most frequent and pressing need for longitudinal data. While there are many groups of stakeholders to be included in the planning phases of the SLDS (statewide longitudinal data system), teachers and administrators will be the two user groups with the most data needs.

The concept of data is not an unfamiliar one to today's teachers. In many schools, they are accustomed to having to track and use data in the classroom. However, longitudinal data, and the volumes of them that an SLDS provides access to, are unlike any data previously used by LEAs (local educational agencies). The effective integration of longitudinal data into schools and the classroom is an important step in realizing the benefits of an SLDS. A true culture of data in schools begins with administrators and teachers. The ultimate purpose of an SLDS is to improve student learning, and this necessitates that teachers welcome and utilize longitudinal data in their day-to-day instruction. It means, also, that teachers and administrators should understand what data will be used, and in what ways, and know that it's not a tool of punishment. While this is, by all measures, a challenging task, establishing a strong culture of data at the school and classroom level is the "final frontier" for the longitudinal data contained in the SLDS. This chapter outlines the culture of data at the school level: key skills for educators and administrators, including classroom data use, and ways to facilitate the culture shift that is necessary to fully utilize longitudinal data. We also discuss the linking of student and teacher records for the purpose of gauging teacher effectiveness. By shifting the focus from numbers and data to student outcomes and the opportunities data provide to better understand each student, schools can change the conversation surrounding data.[1] Demonstrating the value of longitudinal data, the possibilities that exist for educators and administrators to utilize data, ask questions and receive real-time answers that affect learning outcomes for their students, is essential in earning buy-in from this large and crucial set of stakeholders.

Data-driven decision making in education refers to teachers, administrators, local educational agencies (LEAs) and state educational agencies (SEAs) using longitudinal data to help them make choices in and out of the classroom to improve student and school outcomes.[2] Inherent in this process is the ability to take data and transform them into actionable, contextualized information. This chapter details the ways in which longitudinal data can be used to drive student achievement in the classroom and the ways educators can be encouraged and educated to use data to improve their practice. By promoting teachers using data in the classroom and administrators utilizing data and leading the efforts, including linking teacher and student records, we can better evaluate what is working in our educational system and improve it.

TEACHERS

How are longitudinal data different from the data used in classrooms today? Simply put, they enable more context and better decisions. With or without these data, teachers make hundreds of judgments as to how to teach each student, impacting that student's education.[3] Clearly, using data to inform those decisions is a smarter, more accountable way to educate children. Using the longitudinal data made available through statewide efforts and systems provides an unprecedented opportunity to individualize learning and provide greater resources for teachers, if they use the data. The challenge facing states is how to make the data functionally part of classroom and teaching operations.

Having a wealth of longitudinal student information presents amazing possibilities for changing the educational system and the way education is delivered to students. However, data about students do not lead to better outcomes.[4] To be able to utilize longitudinal data educators must be proficient in the following four skills (as shown in Figure 9.1):

1. Ask the right questions.
2. Seek the answers.
3. Interpret and contextualize results.
4. Use information to improve practice.

Each of these abilities needs to be fostered in the teachers of today and tomorrow. It can also be seen as a data-use cycle, wherein as teachers complete the final step and modify their instruction to remediate a need, they continually ask questions and reevaluate the effectiveness of their changes.[5]

Ask the Right Questions

In teacher training programs at universities, rather than having a specific course for using data in the classroom, it should be woven throughout the curriculum. Just as it is (or, in some cases, will be)

Figure 9.1 What Data Skills Do Teachers Need?

in schools, it should be as much a pervasive and indelible part of the teacher training as it is of the teaching profession.

Getting educators to understand, analyze, value and use data begins with schools of education. In 2010, the National Council for the Accreditation of Teacher Education (NCATE) Blue Ribbon Panel updated its recommendations for schools of education to include training on data-driven decision making for pre-service teachers.[6] The suggested inclusion of data integration notes that teachers need to be given training in analyzing data, developing skills and making decisions and "adjust practices using student performance data while receiving continuous monitoring and feedback from mentors."[7]

One part of asking the right questions means understanding what information is contained in the system. Teachers will have access to more longitudinal data than ever before with these initiatives. And it also entails knowing how to ask the right questions of the system, necessitating teacher understanding of how this information can impact their teaching and each student's success. In the example from Chapter 1 where Mrs. Fraser notices her new student, John, lagging in reading for his grade level, the teacher must first know what information is available to her. If longitudinal data from other below-grade level readers' interventions have been assembled to help future cases, it's only truly an aid to future cases if the educators know the data are there and what the data can tell them. The data system might also include a record of past interventions that have been tried with John, which Mrs. Fraser will have to know how to build upon. Further, Mrs. Fraser must know how to ask the system for this information as well. This skill is the result of training and experience in data use. Asking the right questions involves educators having a solid understanding of the system's capabilities and how they relate to their needs.

Seek the Answers

To maximize the potential of access to longitudinal data, teachers are empowered to ask the questions and seek the answers. Each system will be set up differently; teachers could have free access to create reports themselves or be provided with a list of preset queries, or have a data liaison to retrieve all the data they need. While teachers will necessarily be trained and require a level of proficiency in the system, a best practice for reporting within the SLDS is having preset reports that have been deemed useful by teachers. These reports can then be deployed and accessed by the teachers within another system, such as the student information system or the instructional improvement system (IIS). So, rather than having to submit a query for certain parameters monthly, a teacher can choose a saved report structure and run it. The teacher receives this up-to-date information instantly, which is one of the main benefits of an SLDS.

This level of access requires training on the technology for teachers to access the data system holding the longitudinal data. The technology-specific training will most likely come from LEAs, rather than teacher training programs (as there are too many options to expect universities to provide expertise on each). It also requires creativity in seeking the right data that will provide the answer to the question.[8] Using collaborative groups to learn how to better seek the answers that are needed is a suggested method of building this skill.

One of the key advantages of robust SLDSs is that it's possible to survey multiple data sources. Relying on only one source of data, such as a single assessment, skews instruction toward the test material.[9] No single assessment, whether it be a standardized test or other evaluation means, provides teachers with a full picture of the student's learning needs and growth. Using a variety of data sources, for instance, standardized tests, growth data, homework, attendance and unit tests itemized by topic, might help teachers gain more actionable insight. This *triangulation* method of including several sources to produce more valid results is a trusted one among statisticians and researchers, and should be incorporated in educators' use of data as well. In using an SLDS, which by definition includes various data sources, this practice is made simpler.

Interpret and Contextualize Results

It's hard to generalize across systems what form the data will be in when teachers receive them, though it can be assumed that it won't be raw numbers. There will likely be some charts or tables to aid the educator in reading and interpreting the results. It will, however, just be numbers, not prescriptive, actionable information; the results will require a knowledgeable individual to interpret them.[10] In addition to *turning the data into information*, the teachers will then take the information and *place it in context of their classroom* and teaching. Their training in teaching will provide some context, but only if they understand data and statistics as well.

Pedagogical Data Literacy

A fundamental concept in understanding data-driven decision making as it pertains to educators is *pedagogical data literacy*. As defined by Ellen Mandinach, it is "taking data and transforming them into actionable instruction, using pedagogical content knowledge."[11] This concept, that teachers bring their pedagogical expertise to the table and adding data analysis to that skill set only enhances their ability to effectively teach students, is a cornerstone of the SLDS movement. Highlighting teachers' expertise as a key ingredient of data use is essential in this conversation. Sometimes referred to as *instructional decision making*, pedagogical data literacy involves turning data into information and using those results to inform classroom and learning activities.[12] While we know that the level of training teachers receive in schools of training isn't as high as it could be, there are a few accessible skills that are key to fostering this pedagogical data literacy, which ultimately makes longitudinal data useful and impactful for educators. Pedagogical data literacy is the central component when discussing teachers using data in the classroom. Their ability to take numbers and make them into actionable information that informs their instruction is the key issue.[13]

In the process of instituting frequent data usage in the classroom and by educators, it's essential to keep a focus on the professional judgment that teachers, by training, contribute to the equation. The data are provided to enable keener professional judgment. Dr. Jeff Wayman, a foremost researcher in data-driven decision making and education, said, "We don't want to take the professional judgment out of it. In fact, the whole reason we're getting more information and more data is to feed this into their professional judgment and help them make better decisions. Professional judgment is the glue that holds it together."[14] Without the teachers' experiences and expertise, the data are meaningless and lack context. Like all pieces of data inquiry and use for teachers, this skill set and practice must become an integral part of the educator culture.[15]

Use Information to Improve Classroom Practice

Ultimately, the piece of the puzzle that will change outcomes for students is the ability of teachers to use the data they've pulled and information they've learned to individualize learning. SLDS provides reports that will enable easier documentation of student growth and comparison to norms. It provides opportunities for more efficient planning and more targeted instruction.[16]

However, figuring out how to use data to change practice is the most challenging element of educators' use of data in the classroom. After a teacher has successfully asked a relevant question, found the necessary data, interpreted it to a meaningful result, it's time to figure out how the classroom actions and activities are impacting results. This requires a critical and open mind on the part of the educator, and a willingness to consider new approaches. Shaking up the status quo isn't always a popular suggestion among teachers. "We can do something to change how kids are performing, but the reality is, in most cases, teachers in schools have already done their best and what to do differently is a challenge," noted Joan Herman, a teacher.[17] Indeed, Wayman notes that "when we're in the field we see a lot of teachers, almost all teachers, using data, but very rarely do we see some who are adept at changing their practice based on data."[18] All of the previously mentioned data-related skills—asking questions, finding answers and interpreting results—are simple compared to using the data to change the realities of the classroom and student outcomes.

In this particular step, given the complexity of developing this skill set and the importance of it in delivering on the promise of longitudinal data, collaborative learning groups may come in particularly handy. Insights learned through data might include, according to the IES (Institution of Education Sciences) Practice Guide on using student data in the classroom, "allocating more time for topics with which students are struggling; reordering curriculum to shore up essential skills with which students are struggling; designating particular students to receive additional help with particular skills (grouping or regrouping students);

attempting new ways of teaching difficult or complex concepts, especially based on best practices identified by teaching colleagues; better aligning performance expectations among classrooms or between grade levels."[19] There are collaborative uses of the data (changing curriculum and school- or district-wide processes), as well as individual uses for teachers to change their classroom instruction. For this reason, grade-level or departmental working groups can be particularly useful.[20]

So, an added level of complexity is introduced in this step, requiring motivation to change course and correct weaknesses or deficiencies highlighted by the data. An additional benefit to collaborative working groups in learning to turn insight from data into changes in the classroom is the accountability generated from working together, as well as creativity generated from collaboration.

Though there are hard data skills to be added to the teacher's toolbox, a strong teacher with an eye toward professional excellence will see the value and work to cultivate and incorporate these skills in their practice. Longitudinal data offer the ability to make smarter decisions and improve student outcomes, the goals of any good teacher.

ADMINISTRATORS

Though it sounds redundant to say, crucial to the success of the culture of data is the actualization of the data use. While teachers are the group within the schools with the most direct impact on student outcomes, administrators have a huge impact on how teachers use data in practice and in setting the tone for the culture of data within the school or district. For the purposes of this discussion, administrators are most usually principals and superintendents, those roles that manage teachers and schools at the LEA level. In shifting the school-level culture to embrace data-driven decision making, administrators are responsible for encouraging or requiring data use among teachers and using data to evaluate teacher effectiveness. Leadership plays a huge role in effecting change at the school level, setting a clear vision and modeling data use, and making the use of data intrinsic to the culture.[21]

Overall, administrators can facilitate a culture shift at the school level, providing a compelling and overarching vision for school-wide data use. It's important for administrators and leaders to present a persuasive case on what the data can do for teachers and why it is an advantage to them as a classroom tool, to avoid the assumption that data-driven decision making is the next in the line of fads that the education system is trying out. Effective management by administrators can sell educators on the use of longitudinal data as a vital and innovative tool, creating buy-in and interest at all levels and ensuring that the data-related tasks and initiatives aren't imposed upon teachers, but are shaped by them.[22] Continuing to discuss data and reinforce the vision is also very important, proving it is not a passing fad. Principals tend to have higher levels of data literacy, receiving more structured training in administration training programs, and so might be more comfortable incorporating data and sharing it with the organization. A change of this magnitude in school cultural priorities and behavior is a systemic one, requiring all levels within the system to take part.

Encourage or Require Data Use

Administrators are responsible for instituting initiatives that might come from the SEAs, encouraging the use of data in classrooms. This might mean facilitating professional development or workgroups, but also, it entails the ongoing conversation and expectation surrounding data use. Rather than simply decreeing that teachers use the data and not changing anything else surrounding that, administrators need to likewise integrate data into their decisions. If a teacher requests additional resources or suggests a change, data to support that request must be demanded by the administrators before a change is made, reinforcing the importance of data in decision making. Recognizing teachers and workgroups that use data effectively is another way to keep the focus on best practices. Incentivizing effective data use, rewarding teachers who use it well and providing a clear path detailing how teachers can learn to use longitudinal data in their classroom are excellent ways to effectively lead a school to a culture of data.

Evaluating Teachers Using Longitudinal Data

Another key way for administrators to influence the data culture is to use data to evaluate teacher effectiveness and school growth and trends. Seeing aggregated data about entire grades of students could help identify struggling teachers, even pinpointing weaknesses and providing opportunity for intervention before negative student impact is felt. Aggregated data can enable comparisons between teachers, students, demographic groups and many other combinations and impact the way the school operates, and ideally, increase the success of the school. Having access to rich longitudinal data provides opportunities for administrators to more effectively manage educators, and their data use sets the tone for the whole school. The most effective way to do this in an SLDS is to link teacher and student records.

THE TEACHER–STUDENT RECORD LINK

It's hard to match the impact that a great teacher can have on a student. Recent studies have shown that a highly effective teacher can have more impact on students than smaller class size or virtually any other factor.[23] While promoting greater effectiveness in teaching is often touted, data-driven steps toward accomplishing this end are few and far between. The current paradigm for defining, finding and rewarding effective teachers is largely anecdotal. Moreover, without access to timely and reliable data, any steps toward associating teacher effectiveness with student records or outcomes are inherently flawed. There are many possibilities that the use of longitudinal data enables, including the linking of teachers to their students' data, which in turn allows teachers to be evaluated on data beyond standardized tests.

This linkage is controversial and unpopular among educators, fearing their salaries or jobs could be negatively impacted by standardized test scores, a metric many aren't sure is a clear representation of student learning.[24] For many educators, it's hard to see beyond the mental association of merit pay and teacher–student data linking. While the link can certainly be used to institute merit pay (and it might well be used for this purpose), it's not the only manifestation of the link. Regardless, linking the data presents many opportunities that would change the current teacher tenure system. The Gates Foundation advocates for the link, stating, "Many teacher effectiveness reforms rely on innovative practices that represent a major threat to the status quo, such as compensation tied to student achievement growth over time rather than the number of academic degrees a teacher earns or years in the classroom."[25] Gaining teacher buy-in on this idea will, we think, come gradually after some states begin implementing it and using it to positively influence the education system. Objectively evaluating teaching practices based on data is one of the most promising research fields that an SLDS opens up, one that is currently not possible.

U.S. Secretary of Education Arne Duncan said, "We believe great teachers matter tremendously. When you're reluctant or scared to make that link, you do a grave disservice to the teaching profession and to our nation's children."[26] Relying on more than just test data and using systems that supply timely and accurate data provide an opportunity for great teachers to be identified and for schools to increase teacher effectiveness collectively. Learning what works in the classroom, for the first time, is possible through data analysis.

Case Study: New York's Teacher–Student Data Link

The Race to the Top program encourages states to link student and teacher records for evaluation purposes, in some cases tying eligibility for funding to the capability to institute this link.[27] For example, in the New York State Education Department (NYSED), an initiative was undertaken (funded through a 2009 NCES grant) aimed at linking student records to their teachers and using this link for evaluative purposes. As we write this book, it is an unfolding story, with opposition from teachers' unions and various others. It underscores the need for robust student data, not simply standardized test scores, to be connected to teachers, as well as a deep cultural shift for administrators and teachers to view the data as valuable.[28] An SLDS can enable more effective teacher evaluation and a smart merit pay program, if instituted properly. New York's method is one way to establish the link, and, as no two SLDSs are exactly the same, each state will arrive at a different result based upon its circumstances.

New York's Annual Professional Performance Review (APPR) was enacted by Governor Andrew Cuomo in May 2010, compelling LEAs to implement a performance-based evaluation and pay system for teachers and principals.[29] NYSED uses the LEAs to accomplish the needed tasks, building in sustainability and local buy-in to the system. The primary motivation behind the system is to create a better teacher evaluation program linked to data and student achievement. Once in place, the ranking system will label each teacher in the state as "Highly Effective, Effective, Developing, or Ineffective." The ranking will be based on the following formula:

20 percent state assessment

20 percent local achievement

60 percent other (such as administrator classroom evaluation)[30]

Since the evaluations are based on growth and achievement data, limitations exist. State assessments are administered for third-to-eighth-graders, so K–third-grade teachers won't have any scores (or prior-year scores) on which to be evaluated. Additionally, state assessments test English, Language Arts and Math, so teachers of untested subjects aren't able to be ranked using assessment data. Despite these limitations, there are enough data and interest to get started.

New York's Teacher Student Data Link uses three numbers to establish the teacher-of-record relationship. First, it captures the total minutes that the course was in session. Second, it calculates the amount of time the teacher and the student overlapped in the class. This number would be impacted if the teacher was hired midyear or took a leave of absence. Third, it captures the number of minutes the student was in attendance, deducting absences. These three calculations give the system the data to understand how much impact a teacher has had on a student, and how much credit to give the teacher for the student's growth.[31]

This link can be used in many ways, not solely for teacher evaluation as many assume. It will enable schools to keep more thorough rosters, knowing where students are at all moments of the day. This offers tremendous advantages for safety and security reasons. The link allows for systems to more easily define which students teachers have access to within the SLDS, since they're only entitled access to students in their classes, not all students. The link also allows a better process for sharing with parents which teachers their student has, and which teachers and administrators have access to the student's data.[32]

In New York, in the years since 2010, pilot data collections have been under way, and 2012–2013 is the first compulsory year where New York's schools are collecting and linking teachers' and principals' records to the students they're responsible for and to the achievement of the student. A clause for mandatory public reporting of APPR data was added to the law in June 2012, and the first round of data on the pilot group was released in February 2013.[33]

Why the Teacher–Student Record Link Matters

Being able to connect students to the teachers who taught them in the SLDS, thus connecting those teachers with varying levels of success in specific areas, is very relevant to any discussions on teacher effectiveness or training. How do we know what works best? The Data Quality Campaign (DQC) states, "Matching teachers to students by classroom and subject is critical to understanding the connection between teacher training and qualifications and student academic growth."[34] In addition to the obvious benefits, there are very real incentives for states to create these links.

Ultimately, linking student and teacher data is definitely necessary, and as the Gates Foundation says, the "linchpin" to accurately measuring teacher effectiveness.[35] Decisions that are currently made based on assumptions (for instance, that a teacher with a master's degree is more effective) can easily be either confirmed or refuted with hard data. In many ways, this link is the final step to the teacher data-use initiatives discussed earlier in this chapter: Applying data use and evaluation to teacher training and performance completes the culture of data transition. As such, this link should be included in the Governance discussions about the SLDS setup and capabilities.

Best Practices in Implementing the Link

There are several important best practices in establishing and maintaining this link successfully. It's a difficult element of an SLDS to navigate, with competing and conflicting interests from teachers and unions, the federal government and the technical staff. There are many benefits to establishing a clear and reliable teacher–student data link, as we've discussed, and here are some ways to overcome or avoid the challenges and difficulties that might arise.

Clearly Define Teacher Effectiveness and Objectives

Defining what an effective teacher is from the start is essential. Each LEA will have to determine what data will be used to define this measurement, and what practices are exemplary. In many cases, using teacher evaluations and student achievement data will be a good start. Looking at growth in student achievement over time is a major element that should be used in a teacher effectiveness equation.[36]

As the New York case study illustrates, establishing a teacher of record is no easy task and will require some finesse. To establish the link, states will determine what their formula will be for establishing the teacher of record and will define how the data link can be used.[37] Being clear from the beginning that the link is going to be established and what the intentions are behind it will help to create common understanding, and eventually teacher buy-in. "Schools must overcome teachers' distrust and use data not as a hammer, but as a flashlight," said Aimee Guidera, executive director of the DQC.[38] Will the system be used to establish merit-based teacher pay, or to better gauge teacher training and improve the process? Will the system attach only federal standardized test scores to the teacher of record, or are other student data points associated, promoting a deeper understanding of the student and teacher? There are, of course, many rich data connections to be made by a variety of data points (beyond testing data) that not only can enrich the teacher's experience, but can improve education for children.

Teacher UID

The teacher UID (unique identifier) will be set up when the student UID is established, early in the SLDS process as noted in the earlier chapters of this book. Having a solid way to refer to all staff and students, matching records over time, is a key element in any SLDS and especially invaluable in establishing the student–teacher data link.

Collaborate

Setting up the teacher–student record link will be most successful, like almost every element of an SLDS we discuss, if the process includes all levels of stakeholders and offers process ownership for each. It shouldn't be treated as a secretive or technical task, but as one where suggestions are sought and input is valued. It is imperative that educators feel some ownership in the process, as LEAs are often the ones that will be responsible for resolving link-related issues should they arise down the road. Something as simple as a mistaken link between a student and teacher can be easily spotted by the teacher in question. Ideally, teachers should be able to review their rosters to ensure that the system has them linked to the correct students.[39] Additionally, collaborating with the SEA and neighboring districts is useful. The policies and uses of the information gleaned from teacher–student data linkages should be consistent system-wide.

CONCLUSION

A teacher's job is unarguably challenging. They must provide an education for a classroom full of students, using resources that are ever-diminishing, figuring out what each student needs to learn and retain concepts. SLDSs hold the keys to many of these difficult and essential job functions. SLDSs provide an unprecedented opportunity to offer individualized learning, if teachers can use those data to change their instruction. Access to an SLDS enables objective criteria to fuel instructional decisions, rather than intuition or demographic stereotypes.[40] Essentially, an effectively implemented and utilized SLDS, at the school level, provides teachers and administrators with the ability to work smarter, not harder.[41]

Likewise, for administrators, SLDSs offer an unprecedented opportunity to collect and analyze data on teachers, students and programs, and thus evaluate their effectiveness, thereby promoting the collective effectiveness of entire schools and systems through best practices. The culture of data that schools are embracing will encompass all levels of employees and students, and it holds the potential to challenge and improve the quality of all involved. There are many culture-shattering changes to be made to accommodate this shift, and many that are unpopular among educators and administrators. These changes, however, offer a wealth of benefits and advantages and simply cannot be ignored. Training educators for the future of classroom decision making and updating the skills of in-service teachers are crucial steps in leveraging the power of the SLDS.

NOTES

1. Brad C. Phillips and Jay J. Pfeiffer, "Commentary: Dear Data, Please Make Yourself More Useful," EdWeek Online, http://www.edweek.org/ew/articles/2012/05/23/32phillips.h31.html, May 22, 2012 (accessed July 18, 2012).

2. Julie A. Marsh, John F. Pane, and Laura S. Hamilton, "Making Sense of Data-Driven Decision Making in Education," 2006, Rand Education, http://www.rand.org/pubs/occasional_papers/2006/RAND_OP170.pdf (accessed August 8, 2012).

3. U.S. Department of Education, "Teachers' Ability to Use Data to Inform Instruction: Challenges and Supports," prepared by Barbara Means, Eva Chen, Angela DeBarger, and Christine Padilla (2011).

4. Ibid.

5. Institute of Educational Services, "Using Student Achievement Data to Support Instructional Decision Making," IES Practice Guide (2009).

6. Ellen B. Mandinach, Edith S. Gummer, and Robert D. Muller, "The Complexities of Integrating Data-Driven Decision Making into Professional Preparation in Schools of Education: It's Harder Than You Think," report from an Invitational Meeting, May 12, 2011.

7. National Council for Accreditation of Teacher Education, "Transforming Teacher Education through Clinical Practice: A National Strategy to Prepare Effective Teachers," http://www.ncate.org/LinkClick.aspx?fileticket=zzeiB1OoqPk%3D&tabid=715 (accessed August 8, 2012).

8. Ellen B. Mandinach, Edith S. Gummer, and Robert D. Muller, "The Complexities of Integrating Data-Driven Decision Making into Professional Preparation in Schools of Education."

9. Institute of Educational Services, "Using Student Achievement Data to Support Instructional Decision Making."

10. Hasmik J. Danielian, "District Level Practices in Data Driven Decision Making," Ph.D. dissertation, University of Southern California, Los Angeles, May 2009, http://digitallibrary.usc.edu/cdm/ref/collection/p15799coll127/id/208280.

11. Ellen B. Mandinach, Edith S. Gummer, and Robert D. Muller, "The Complexities of Integrating Data-Driven Decision Making into Professional Preparation in Schools of Education."

12. Ibid.

13. Ibid.

14. Ibid.

15. Ibid.

16. Ibid.

17. Ibid.

18. Ibid.

19. Institute of Educational Services, "Using Student Achievement Data to Support Instructional Decision Making."

20. Ibid.

21. Hasmik J. Danielian, "District Level Practices in Data Driven Decision Making."

22. Institute of Educational Services, "Using Student Achievement Data to Support Instructional Decision Making."

23. Bill and Melinda Gates Foundation, "Empowering Effective Teachers: Readiness for Reform," issue brief (February 2012).

24. Emily Alpert, "New Number-Crunching Links Teachers to Test Scores," http://www.voiceofsandiego.org/education/article_b4974861-c8c3-5858-a5d8-4c81b09ac0f8.html (accessed August 8, 2012).

25. Bill and Melinda Gates Foundation, "Empowering Effective Teachers."

26. Michele McNeil, "'Race to Top' Guidelines Stress Use of Test Data," *Education Week*, July 23, 2009, http://www.edweek.org/ew/articles/2009/07/23/37race.h28.html (accessed May 23, 2013).

27. Ellen B. Mandinach, Edith S. Gummer, and Robert D. Muller, "The Complexities of Integrating Data-Driven Decision Making into Professional Preparation in Schools of Education."

28. Jenny Anderson, "Curious Grade for Teachers," March 30, 2013, http://www.nytimes.com/2013/03/31/education/curious-grade-for-teachers-nearly-all-pass.html (accessed May 2, 2013).

29. NYSED, Race to the Top, "Guidance for the Field," http://usny.nysed.gov/rttt/teachers-leaders/fieldguidance/ (accessed February 20, 2013).

30. Charlene Swanson, Data Quality Coordinator NYSED, interview with author, February 19, 2013.

31. Ibid.

32. Ibid.

33. Ibid.

34. Data Quality Campaign, "10 Essential Elements of a State Longitudinal Data System," http://dataqualitycampaign.org/build/elements/5/ (accessed August 1, 2012).

35. Bill and Melinda Gates Foundation, "Empowering Effective Teachers."

36. Ibid.

37. Data Quality Campaign, "Effectively Linking Teacher and Student Data: The Key to Improving Teacher Quality," July 2010, http://www.dataqualitycampaign.org/resources/details/993 (accessed August 8, 2012).

38. Emily Alpert, "New Number-Crunching."

39. Data Quality Campaign, "Effectively Linking Teacher and Student Data."

40. U.S. Department of Education, "Teachers' Ability to Use Data to Inform Instruction."

41. Rhonda Barton, "Fostering a Data-Driven Culture," *Education Northwest* 16, no. 2 (2011): 6–9, http://educationnorthwest.org/webfm_send/1130.

CHAPTER 10

Expanding Your SLDS: Adding Out-of-School Time and Health-Care Data

Longitudinal data on each student, detailing academic and testing information from preschool through K–12 and beyond, present an important step forward for most data systems and enable new and useful research to be done. However, it still doesn't present the most comprehensive view of each child. To gain insight into each child's situation—the complex interplay of all of the factors in the student's world that might encourage or inhibit academic success—still more data must be included in the longitudinal data system. Many other data systems, such as health and human services, juvenile justice and social services, can be linked to provide a better view of the student. In this chapter, we discuss two vital datasets necessary to get a *360° view* of the child: out-of-school time (OST) and health-care data.

Out-of-school time (OST) data detail what students do when they're not in school. While much can be done (and *is* done) in the classroom to prepare students to succeed in college and in a career, there are only seven hours in the school day, and what happens in those hours not spent in school can impact a student's outcome. According to IES

(Institute of Education Sciences), OST is "an opportunity to supplement learning from the school day and provide targeted assistance to students whose needs extend beyond what they can receive in the classroom."[1] Further, knowledge of what goes on after school could positively impact the education a student receives in the form of timely interventions, remediation or other recommendations. Currently, these OST programs, like afterschool programs, summer and holiday programs and community aid (in the form of weekend food assistance and other programs), are largely unconnected to the P20 student record file (if one exists). For older students, OST includes internships, jobs and service learning placements as well.[2] If a behavior incident is noted after school, or a family situation discovered by someone outside of the school system, the student's K–12 record is unaffected, and his teachers left unaware. Likewise, if an afterschool program is helping a child with certain concepts and his grades are improving, no feedback is given to the afterschool program that their efforts are paying off. This lack of connectedness leaves many gaps in information, giving educators a fraction of the picture. (See Figure 10.1.)

Data regarding the student's health and wellness, or *health-care data*, also hold useful insight that could further inform the picture of the whole student. Providing more details about a student's educationally relevant health issues would provide the opportunity for administrators to better address those needs, or to see collectively that a school is failing to meet certain types of needs. Data about vision exams, inattention and hyperactivity and physical activity levels, for example, would add to the breadth of data available to researchers and educators, and provide opportunities for richer insights into what enables or prevents success in learning. Further, it would enable the delivery of better health services to children. In many recent studies, it's been shown that healthier students learn better and thrive academically.[3]

Among OST, health programs and other related data systems, data can be shared to identify gaps in service or overlaps and to ensure that community resources are maximized. These connections need to be made. For the teachers and administrators, these data could help paint a clearer picture of the student. Currently, the OST data points are out there, though in most cases that means in the heads of the program administrators and not in a formalized database. To be useful,

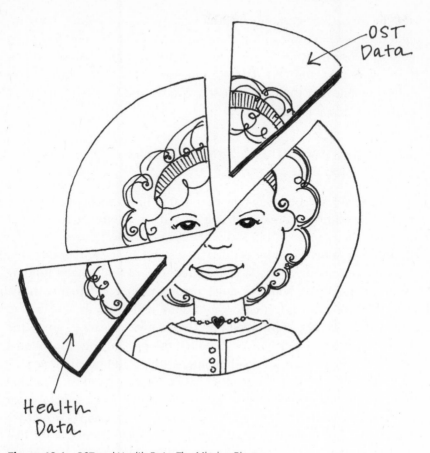

Figure 10.1 OST and Health Data: The Missing Pieces

they must be connected to student records within a longitudinal data system. While these connections are several years in the future—OST data systems lag behind educational data systems—we see it as vital that they be considered as relevant and the next step for any developing and growing SLDS.

We are spending a lot of money and time focusing on these issues collectively. As a country we know that students' health and wellness affects their learning, and that these issues compound and cost the system precious resources. Including more related data in SLDSs is the only way we can gain a clear picture of the whole student, learning what factors affect learning and influence success or failure. Longitudinal data are key to learning about academic success, and including more data on the student can lead to better decisions and outcomes. Health-care data and OST data are integral pieces of the puzzle. This chapter details why these data are so valuable, and how states can plan for their eventual inclusion.

COLLECTIVE IMPACT: THE LONGITUDINAL DATA CONNECTION

Collective impact is a good way to conceptualize how touchpoints in each child's education are organized and shared, as identified by Kramer and Kania in a *Stanford Social Innovation Review* article.[4] Currently, most education systems could be defined as systems of *isolated impact*. That is, discussions about success are "oriented toward finding and funding a solution embodied within a single organization, combined with the hope that the most effective organizations will grow or replicate to extend their impact more widely."[5] This is not surprising, given the limited resources available for funding nonprofits and educational programs. But this sort of methodology—only funding the one program that is most impactful—is not as effective as it could be. Thinking about it in terms of medicine is illustrative. If one were searching for a cure for a complex and pervasive disease, such as cancer, would we assume there was one drug to cure every form and instance of the disease? Of course not; we know there are different types of cancer, and different treatments and drugs affect them differently. Similarly, when searching out reasons a school or group of students is failing, it is naïve to assume there is one action or organization that can effect enough change to cure the problem, and further, be mass produced to cure all failing schools. But this is precisely the approach that isolated impact uses, seeking the one factor that is positively impacting schools and populations to channel more funding and promote replication, according to Kania and Kramer. The effect of making each educational program compete for limited resources is that many groups are trying to come up with solutions to the same pervasive problems independently, "often working at odds with each other and exponentially increasing the perceived resources required to make meaningful progress."[6]

Certainly, isolated impact does not sound like an ideal way to go about addressing complex and multidimensional problems. Though it is the de facto method used by most education systems, collective impact offers more opportunities for success. Collective impact, according to Kania and Kramer, is defined as "the commitment of a group of important actors from different sectors to a common agenda for solving a specific social problem."[7] So, for OST programs, rather than having afterschool programs compete for funds based on which is the most effective, a collective impact initiative would fund a collaboration among all community stakeholders (including schools and educators) to incentivize solving the problem together. Contrasted to most collaborations, collective impact groups will boast "a centralized infrastructure, a dedicated staff, and a structured process that leads to a common agenda, shared measurement, continuous communication and mutually reinforcing activities among participants."[8] These efforts are suggested for complex issues in a society, of which educational systems are certainly one, and can bring large-scale social change from these cross-sector partnerships. It is easy to see how the inclusion of health-care data and OST data could enrich the ability of schools to have greater impact on students.

While longitudinal data, or SLDSs, are not a prerequisite for creating a collective impact initiative, they certainly make them easier and more effective. Indeed, working with longitudinal data makes for richer, more accurate insights and connectivity to an SLDS provides the opportunity for those insights to be shared, impacting more student outcomes.

OST: WHAT HAPPENS WHEN THEY'RE NOT IN SCHOOL?

When the school bell rings at 3:00 P.M., there are still several hours for most children until their parent(s) take over in their care. While it was recently found that 8.4 million children are enrolled in afterschool programs, 15 million children (more than a quarter of American children) are unsupervised after school.[9] OST includes these before- and afterschool hours as well as summer and holiday breaks, and these data are largely unavailable to longitudinal data systems and educators.

The Forum of Youth Investment (the Forum) focuses a lot of its efforts on the OST issue through its Ready by 21 (RB21) initiative. RB21 is a "set of innovative strategies developed by the Forum that help communities improve the odds that all children and youth will be ready for college, work and life" by helping community partnerships take a whole child/whole community approach to planning, program implementation and impact evaluation.[10] RB21 "provides clear standards to achieve collective impact, tools and solutions to help leaders make progress, and ways to measure and track success along the way at both the community and the program level."[11] RB21 focuses on encouraging leaders to build broader partnerships, set bigger goals, and collect and use better data. They want leaders to take bolder actions to improve all of the systems and settings in which students spend their time and improve all student outcomes: academic, health, and social.

Only half of a student's waking hours are spent in the classroom; what goes on the rest of the day is "off the record."[12] Clearly, this segment of time is important and uncharted. It's hard to have a full picture of children without knowing how they spend the majority of their time. Teachers tend to tell similar stories, according to the Forum's president and CEO, Karen Pittman. A lot can happen in the hours between when school ends and school begins that can either support learning or derail it. There are things that teachers and schools do to anticipate the problems, such as noticing red flags, sending home food packs, and connecting students with mentors or afterschool programs. But by and large, without data and partners, these critical hours are a black box that leaves teachers reacting to problems and not proactively solving them.[13]

"The bottom line is kids don't come in pieces. And the past several decades have taught us that delivering piecemeal solutions isn't giving us the results we need," RB21 said in a recent presentation. "It doesn't matter how much money we invest in independent programs, how many new policies we create, how many partnerships or task forces we convene. Until we fix that messy picture, we're never going to get better results. So, it's time for a change."[14] This sentiment is applicable to most segments in the education system. It speaks to the urgent need for more data and coalitions and task forces focused on a range of child and youth issues, and to the very unification of education data.

There is a growing interest in OST, and specifically, using OST as an opportunity to continue learning activities, potentially bridging the gap between low- and high-achieving students.[15] Research indicates that OST is a time when the achievement gap can grow wider. Not all OST programs have the same goals and structure. Most afterschool programs provide a place for students to safely stay occupied until their parents are done working.[16] Increasingly, however, some programs are being designed to support student success. Some approach this directly by providing academic support; some programs approach this end by cultivating the child's leadership, recreational skills or some combination of other skills.[17] The most important thing OST programs can provide, however, is a quality environment for experience-based learning. Research shows that students who attend high-quality afterschool programs, regardless of their content focus, have higher academic, social and emotional skills than those who attend poor-quality programs.

Funding for OST programs is on the rise, even in the face of ever-diminishing budgets for schools and education. NCLB (No Child Left Behind) required districts to spend 5–20 percent of all of their Title I funds on supplemental educational services (SESs), of which OST is one. The increasing popularity of extending the school day threatens to diminish funding (and use) of OST programs, though this is still in flux at the time of publishing this book.[18] Although OST programs are prevalent in communities nationwide, there is little consensus about which programs are most effective at impacting student achievement. Though we can assume some structured activity is better than none for school-aged children without parental care after school, we don't have much research or common understanding on the best structures for these programs, or standards by which we gauge success.[19] Not having these OST data connected to the student record, or in a unified and connected format, also presents a huge hurdle in establishing any authoritative research on the subject. Each community and state has volumes of afterschool programs, many with intentions of troubleshooting minority and at-risk populations, or aiming to improve student achievement and success as a whole. Currently, the data capabilities to evaluate the effectiveness of programs in real time and to increase pervasiveness of ones that work and curb less effective programs simply don't exist. Broadly speaking, there is also a deficit of conventional wisdom on attracting and retaining participation from at-risk youth in OST programs.[20]

Without a uniform data system, decisions regarding funding and human resources as well as evaluations of success or failure of programs will continue to be made based on anecdotal evidence and hunches. Attaching OST data to a state's LDS would provide three key opportunities for these very valuable data:

1. To define and refine successful OST programs and allocate resources accordingly.
2. To see OST programs' impact more precisely on the student's educational performance.
3. To unify the school and OST program efforts to ensure that the children are being sufficiently prepared to succeed in college, work and life, with OST and school learning coordinated to meet that goal.

In studies involving surveys of employers on the readiness of high school graduates to join the workforce, it was found that while many students are graduating with satisfactory academic skills, the other factors employers were looking for were largely unaddressed by the K–12 system. Beyond passing grades and a diploma, employers are also looking for students with skills such as financial literacy, the ability to solve conflicts diplomatically, time management, decision making, social adjustment, and so on. Employers, when surveyed, report that only 40 percent of high school graduates are coming to them to their standards.[21] In other words, most are not ready for a career or higher education upon graduating. Clearly, this issue goes beyond academics; a high school diploma alone doesn't prepare a student for success in the real world. If schools focus only on testing scores, passing grades and academics, it's not enough to make a child succeed in work and life out of school.[22] "Part of the problem is schools are not using most of the things real-world people are using to evaluate success," Pittman says.[23]

A P20 SLDS, as described in this book and by definition, addresses only a portion of the crucial longitudinal data needed to create a full picture of the student. Inclusion of OST (and health-care data, as discussed ahead) will provide a more robust and actionable dataset, completing the picture of the student, enabling states to have adequate volumes of data to move into the predictive space in educational data modeling.

If we acknowledge that every youth inherently has some capacity to succeed and to struggle as they go through their K–12 years, a greater body of research that uses longitudinal data can only help us to better understand the impact of influences, programs, risk factors and activities on young people. The potential of all youths should be maximized, dramatically lowering the risk for serious difficulties and increasing the rates of success in adulthood.[24]

No matter what the politics, funding or limitations are of a community, all members should agree that it's in the collective interest of society for young people to be prepared to be independent and successful in their post–high school lives. Simply ignoring or disregarding OST data as peripheral to an SLDS project is a mistake. Inclusion in the SLDS holds special opportunity for this dataset, one with mutual benefit for OST programs and the educational system as a whole.

HEALTH-CARE DATA

The link between learning and health is clear, according to the Healthy Schools Campaign, which advocates for increased attention to student wellness and the linkage of health data to student records. It is logical and proven that healthy, well students perform better in the classroom. However, today's schools and data systems do not make that logical connection. Several key health-care data points are documented in the CEDS (Common Education Data Standards) data dictionary, such as vision, dental, and disability; however, it is unclear how they're used and shared currently. FERPA (Family Educational Rights and Privacy Act) and HIPAA (Health Insurance Portability and Accountability Act) present restrictions on the use and dissemination of these data, though there are still many legal ways to include them in the student record while protecting student privacy. Health-care data present many challenges to SLDS administrators, but they also present an opportunity to round out the picture of each student and more effectively deliver education and health services to those in need.

Growing evidence reinforces the connection between health factors and academic success, and a recent report by Dr. Charles Basch surveys this research to link health disparities to the minority achievement gap.[25] Without system-wide acknowledgment of the impact educationally relevant health data can have on a student's ability to succeed in school, efficient delivery of services and education to children will not be possible. Further, Basch's study focuses on the link between health disparities among minorities and the achievement gap in the same group. Any true school reform would need to address the achievement gap among minority populations; addressing health issues (which disproportionately affect minorities) is an indelible part of any such effort.

Basch notes that most schools are "already devoting some attention and resources to addressing important health barriers to learning, but these efforts are too often poor quality, not strategically planned to influence educational outcomes, and not effectively coordinated to maximize linkages between different school health components."[26] In essence, as with the philosophy behind SLDS that linking the data can lead to more efficient use of resources and better outcomes, Basch notes that including health data in student records can lead to more efficient delivery of health services, enabling healthier students, who are in turn more successful in school. To truly support learning and provide the information necessary to get a full picture of what is going on with the student, this link is crucial.

Certainly not all health-care data are, as Basch terms it, "educationally relevant." Including only necessary and relevant data points as they relate to a child's education and learning is a key point. There are several prominent health issues that have been found to impact a student's ability to learn in major ways, Basch points out, and they are good datasets to start with. (See Figure 10.2.) Vision, asthma, teen pregnancy, aggression and violence, physical activity, breakfast and inattention and hyperactivity are the most impactful and relevant health-care datasets that could influence the education a child receives.[27] Indeed, if intervention doesn't take place in a timely fashion, the child's early educational foundations can be impacted, which can be a huge handicap as he attempts future academic success. If he can't see to learn his letters and learn to read in elementary school, how will he succeed in high school?

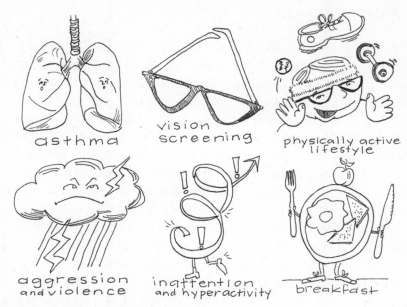

asthma

vision screening

physically active lifestyle

aggression and violence

inattention and hyperactivity

breakfast

Figure 10.2 Educationally Relevant Health Data

Health-related problems have a major impact on motivation and the ability to learn successfully.[28] Tracking health data and intervening to improve child health and wellness can serve the dual purpose of improving health and education. With health issues persisting and growing, even more so among poor and minority populations, investments in educational initiatives will be profoundly limited if attention is not paid to the health of students. SLDSs offer an opportunity to include these data and make connections where they were not possible before. Strategically linking health data to educational data will serve to maximize the impact of resources in the educational system. Basch notes that "a substantial investment in health related programs and services already exists in the nation's schools. But because these current programs are categorical and fragmented rather than strategic and coordinated the return on investment is limited."[29] In short, the efforts to stem these health problems aren't strategically planned or tracked, so there's no way to improve them over time or associate them with educational outcomes.

FERPA Compliance

Connecting educationally relevant health data to the student record brings up many issues relating to FERPA, HIPAA or both. Schools are hesitant to enter this realm because of the myriad restrictions that are placed on them in regard to the ways in which this information is handled and shared. Some states pose more limiting laws relating to student health data storage and sharing, going beyond what FERPA and HIPAA limit. "State law can be more restrictive than FERPA, but it can't be less restrictive than FERPA. In other words, FERPA sets the bar on privacy," according to Baron Rodriguez, director of the Privacy Technical Assistance Center (PTAC).[30] While there are many caveats, establishing this link is a worthwhile endeavor and is legal. Interagency data sharing is something an SLDS should be built to facilitate, and new SLDS administrators should investigate their state's particular laws pertaining to student health data.

CEDS offers data fields relating to each of the seven key academically relevant health-care data fields that Basch defined. For instance, in regard to the student's vision, the Vision Screening field provides a place for the results of an exam (field number 000308), and the Vision Screening Date field holds the "year, month and day of a vision screening" (field number 000703).[31] Associating these data with a child's student record is possible, but making the required connections and taking actions, for use either within the school or by researchers, is necessary to make the data informative and useful. Tracking the data is a start, but making the connections and using the data to inform decisions and instruction is the ultimate goal for health-care data.

As with all student data, keeping student privacy and data security in mind is paramount. Any health-care data will be subject to the same procedures as any other data fields as far as public disclosure and sharing among agencies goes, as established by Governance. Keep in mind the idea of user access levels, a key component of all SLDSs. All users will not have access to all data. This is certainly true of health-care data that might be linked to the student record. It's important to remember that when a link is discussed, it is not one with wide access that would necessarily breach privacy laws.

HOW TO FACILITATE COLLECTIVE IMPACT INITIATIVES

Moves to include health-care data and OST data in an SLDS are, essentially, collective impact initiatives. Including health and OST data in the student record acknowledges that there are many factors influencing each child, more than simply academic information that will give a clear picture of what is going on in his life. They also recognize that there is no magic solution for every community to make it a safe, happy place for children; there is no single organization that can meet every different community's needs.[32] To be sure, incorporating a full 360° view of the student is the only way to track and learn about the myriad factors that impact his success or failure. Seeing the data picture as more expansive and inclusive can only help a longitudinal data system to be built to meet the growing needs of a community and educational system. While the realization of the inclusion of these datasets is several years out, it is important to keep an eye toward this expansion.

The ability of an SLDS to be fully utilized in this way is predicated on the inclusion of OST and educationally relevant health data. Pittman suggests beginning the design and discussions surrounding inclusion of OST data with what you want to know in the end. In other words, start with the child and the desired output of data and connections and develop the system accordingly. By beginning the exercise by defining the ideal outcome, a state can then backtrack to make sure that the essential skills are being taught and tracked in their data system.[33] The key data providers that hold the data required will need to be included to enable the robust system and results desired.

Starting with the child forces something else: It compels stakeholders and communities to think about all of the issues a child may experience and all of the agencies that the child might be involved with rather than just one.[34] It further promotes seeing these issues as interconnected. Kania and Kramer present five conditions for collective success in community partnerships:

1. Common agenda
2. Shared measurement systems
3. Mutually reinforcing activities

4. Continuous communication

5. Backbone support organizations[35]

These best practices more or less mirror RB21's mission, and provide some insight into the importance of a collaborative effort in building bridges between SLDSs and new datasets. Promoting discussion and objective reflection on services provided and student outcome is crucial to the success of a collaborative effort.

In Cincinnati and northern Kentucky, the Strive Network has emerged as an example of a successful collective impact initiative that involves a balanced set of goals. The Strive Network has been distinguished by its high levels of involvement from area leaders and their collective approach to solving the pervasive youth and educational issues they are facing as a community. Rather than focusing on one aspect of the educational continuum, they choose to focus on every stage of the student's life. This holistic approach centers around a common set of goals and trackers to measure success. It tracks several student factors, including high school graduation rates, Kindergarten preparedness and so on, showing growth in 34 of the 53 indicators in the years since its inception—a huge accomplishment.[36] The Strive Network is a prime example of how working together collectively can make difficult social and educational problems solvable.

Currently, buy-in on collective impact as a means for improving the education system seems to be high. People may say they agree in theory; however, there are several significant hurdles to establishing a functioning and effective collaborative effort. "Attempting to 'rewire' a community for collective impact without the necessary capacity or with inadequate tools is a recipe for failure that leads to complacency, further fragmentation and low expectations for change."[37] And when we're talking about restructuring collaborative efforts to allow for collective impact, the SLDS initiative provides an opening to accomplish just that. SLDSs, the technology that tracks and makes available longitudinal data, make this sort of collaboration possible and attainable, and thus all of the benefits of collective impact within reach. Including OST and health-care data in an SLDS is feasible and a recommended next step for those systems that are already in place. For new systems, inclusion is a best practice.

To foster these collaborations that include OST and health data, several steps are suggested.

1. Define the organizations that make up the community. Determining the list of stakeholders is a key exercise (i.e., YMCA, Boys and Girls Clubs and afterschool programs, sports activities, mentoring/academic programs, schools). While it might sound basic, defining *community* can be challenging, and defining *stakeholders* is crucial to fostering accountability in developing solutions.

2. Obtain MOUs from each stakeholding party, committing them to involvement in the effort and to share data with each other. This action also invests stakeholder agencies in the partnership. OST programs will form a sort of network, connected to one another and to the educational data system.

3. Define each organization, itemizing who it serves, how many children it serves and what data it will bring to the table. There are often layers of complexity in this step; sometimes, it's hard to know how many kids are served.

   For example, Karen Pittman tells a story about a community organization that was found to serve 3,500 children after an audit was performed. When the board and stakeholders of that organization were asked how many students were served, they estimated 10,000.[38] This disparity, sadly, is not uncommon, making this step crucial in getting a clear picture of each agency's reach. "Whereas the challenges for schools relate to meaningful reform," says Pittman, "the challenges for out-of-school and community-based learning are creating 'form' in the first place."[39]

4. Get each agency's data in the same, compatible format. Similar to how each education partner will map their data to CEDS and use student UIDs (unique identifiers), the OST and health data network must fall in line with the SLDS and its data requirements to enable a bridge to the SLDS to be established.

5. Establish the connection to school data, with OST and health-care systems sending data to the SLDS and utilizing data they need access to.

6. Use the SLDS and learn more about the impact of every educational influence on each student.

Ultimately, in including OST and health data, it's important to meet leaders where they are. Instead of blowing up what exists, figure out how the existing SLDS can be leveraged to be more useful and include more data, positioning the expansion as a way to make the SLDS more useful. When a state is building a new system, try to include OST and health data provisions early in the process, ensuring there is room to include these data in the future.

Also note that the previous list can be ongoing and isn't necessarily comprehensive for all communities. While it is probably unreasonable to expect a brand-new SLDS to include afterschool program data initially, the OST agencies and community stakeholders can and should begin getting their data collections initialized and taking care to keep them in good condition. Facilitating evaluations and documenting results with an eye toward gathering enough information to make predictive analysis is a best practice in any event, especially so when inclusion in an SLDS is a possibility.

In the end, "we have to help leaders see what is possible," RB21's Pittman says. All of the things we've discussed in the book so far—complex data systems, new analysis to improve the system as a whole and inclusion of new related datasets—may not be welcome changes by all parties. It means more work. It means opening up the doors to inspection of data and practices and criticism. It's the responsibility of those involved to inspire leaders to see that current outcomes are not acceptable. A laundry list of health issues—asthma, vision problems, attention-deficit/hyperactivity disorder (ADHD)—negatively impact the ability of children to thrive in schools and disproportionally affect urban minorities.[40] This is objectively unacceptable, but bringing these discrepancies to light is the only way to create awareness and motivation to change. The next step is inspiring leaders to look at the information differently and see that educational and school data alone aren't providing enough context for a full picture of the child and his experience.

CONCLUSION

It is clear that to change the situation for today's youth it will take investment from a broad range of community leaders and educational stakeholders.[41] Our data systems and our educational systems are undergoing vital and necessary changes currently, and it's important to include a breadth of stakeholders and data in those decisions. While the datasets discussed in this chapter mostly present future areas for expansion and systems that are not yet mature enough to be connected to SLDSs, giving these stakeholders a place at the table in SLDS discussions is a best practice. Developing SLDSs to eventually include these data and thinking in terms of the whole child is the only way to maximize the utilization of educational resources.

NOTES

1. IES: National Center for Education Evaluation and Regional Assistance, "Structuring Out-of-School Time to Improve Academic Achievement," Best Practice Guide (July 2009).
2. Karen Pittman, personal notes (July 23, 2013).
3. Charles E. Basch, "Healthier Students Are Better Learners: A Missing Link in School Reforms to Close the Achievement Gap," *Equity Matters: Research Review*, no. 6 (March 2010), Campaign for Educational Equity, Teachers College, Columbia University.
4. John Kania and Mark Kramer, "Collective Impact," *Stanford Social Innovation Review*, Winter 2011, http://www.ssireview.org/articles/entry/collective_impact (accessed April 23, 2012).
5. Ibid.
6. Ibid.
7. Ibid.
8. Ibid.
9. Afterschool Alliance, "Facts and Research," http://www.afterschoolalliance.org/AA3PM.cfm (accessed July 25, 2013).
10. Ready by 21, "Strategy Presentation" (February 22, 2012).
11. Ready by 21, "The Problem," http://www.readyby21.org/what-ready-21/problem (accessed June 22, 2012).
12. S. L. Hofferth and J. F. Sandberg, "How American Children Spend Their Time," *Journal of Marriage and Family* 63, no. 2 (2001): 295–308.
13. Karen Pittman, interview with author, May 11, 2012.
14. Ready by 21, "Strategy Presentation."
15. R. Halpern, After-School Programs for Low-Income Children: Promise and Challenges," *The Future of Children* 9, no. 2 (1999): 81–95.
16. IES: National Center for Education Evaluation and Regional Assistance, "Structuring Out-of-School Time to Improve Academic Achievement."
17. Forum for Youth Investment and University of Chicago, "From Soft Skills to Hard Data: Measuring Youth Program Outcomes" (October 2011).
18. Valerie Strauss, "The Secret War on Afterschool Programs," *Washington Post*, July 15, 2013, http://www.washingtonpost.com/blogs/answer-sheet/wp/2013/07/15/the-secret-war-on-afterschool-programs/ (accessed July 24, 2013).

19. IES: National Center for Education Evaluation and Regional Assistance, "Structuring Out-of-School Time to Improve Academic Achievement."

20. "Study of Predictors of Participation in OST Activities," Harvard Family Research Project, http://www.hfrp.org/out-of-school-time/projects/study-of-predictors-of-participation-in-out-of-school-time-activities (accessed June 21, 2012).

21. Jill Casner-Lotto, Linda Barrington, and Mary Wright, "Are They Really Ready to Work?" The Conference Board, May 2006, http://www.conference-board.org/publications/publicationdetail.cfm?publicationid=1494 (accessed July 23, 2013).

22. Karen Pittman, interview.

23. Ibid.

24. Michelle Alberti Gambone, Adena M. Klem, and James P. Connell, "Finding Out What Matters for Youth: Testing Key Links in a Community Action Framework for Youth Development," Youth Development Strategies Inc. and Institute for Research and Reform in Education (November 2002).

25. Healthy Schools Campaign, "Health in Mind: Improving Education Through Wellness," http://www.healthyschoolscampaign.org/news/new-report-calls-for-federal-action-to-close-achievement-gap-by-addressing/ (accessed June 21, 2012).

26. Charles E. Basch, "Healthier Students Are Better Learners."

27. Ibid.

28. Ibid.

29. Ibid.

30. Baron Rodriguez, interview with author, May 2012.

31. CEDS, "Common Education Data Standards (CEDS) Version 2 Data Model Guide," January 31, 2012, https://ceds.ed.gov/pdf/ceds-data-model-guide.pdf (accessed August 9, 2012).

32. Ready by 21, "Strategy Presentation."

33. Karen Pittman, interview.

34. Community Level Interventions, "Ready by 21: A Summary of Relevant Research" (no year noted).

35. John Kania and Mark Kramer, "Collective Impact."

36. Ibid.

37. Ready by 21, "Strategy Presentation."

38. Karen Pittman, interview.

39. Ibid.

40. Charles E. Basch, "Healthier Students Are Better Learners."

41. Ready by 21, "Strategy Presentation."

CHAPTER **11**

A Culture of Data: Using Longitudinal Data to Solve Big Problems

As hard as it is to establish and implement an SLDS (statewide longitudinal data system), it's "easier than changing how people value and use education data," according to the Data Quality Campaign (DQC).[1] Changing the organizational culture of schools is a huge task, but it's an important one to make to fully realize the potential of an SLDS. This shift is systemic in nature, meaning every part of the system is affected and must move in the same direction together. Reliance on one part of the system doesn't lead to success; it requires thinking of each of the recommendations and steps in creating an SLDS as interdependent and important. The burden for a dramatic cultural shift belongs on all of the parts of the system. Likewise, though this book is dealing with statewide LDSs, we recognize that the way data are treated at the school level has a substantial impact on teacher data use, and cultures can vary widely from school to school. Administrators have a powerful role and responsibility to lead the school toward a culture of data; data literacy at the leadership level holds great potential in ushering in a new era of decision making. Creating a culture of data for educators and administrators is an ongoing task, forcing the system to embrace change and technology while repudiating the status quo. Proactive data usage enables more accurate warning systems, better individual outcomes and a better microscope on what is working in education. Creating a culture of data is a vital change for the education system as a whole in the coming years; in today's information-driven climate, it is no longer an option to make decisions without data.

In this chapter, we discuss the culture of data from a human perspective: How do administrators and teachers make changes at the school level to facilitate the culture-of-data mentality and incorporate data-driven decision making into their day-to-day job? We also discuss the tools at their disposal that can work with SLDSs to enable the key connections to be made, making the longitudinal data useful; actionable data feed the culture of data.

CREATING A CULTURE OF DATA

To set up the SLDS for success at the school level, changes to the way data are managed, discussed and used must be made by both administrators and teachers. Data use is becoming more and more a daily reality for teachers, so while it is not new, there are very real misconceptions and negative experiences to be overcome.[2] Part of making sure the SLDS is different—a game-changer—is to make sure the culture is prepared to accommodate it. To effectively create a culture that embraces data-driven decisions (Figure 11.1), it is essential to foster trust in the data efficacy and the process, be clear about what the data are used for, use data often and take part in professional development to learn and maintain the right skills.

Leadership

We discuss leadership at the state level in this book a lot. It is vitally important to have strong governance and state leaders steering the SLDS project and communicating its progress and mission. Local leaders

Figure 11.1 Creating a Culture of Data

at the LEA (local education agency) level are equally vital to the implementation of a culture of data use. Those leading the longitudinal data use initiatives at the local level should communicate a clear vision. Utilizing longitudinal data in decision making represents a huge shift in behavior and organizational culture, and leaders must clearly communicate what the goal is.[3] Their vision should be discussed frequently and backed up by policy initiatives that reinforce behavioral changes and reward good data use. In any shift to data-driven culture, if the buy-in and vision do not guide the group toward the new procedures and shifts, there is a risk that the project will fail. Strong leadership will provide the momentum for the project and for all of the other ways to establish a culture of data.

Local leaders also have the important role of enabling greater data use within the schools. If there are established policies that reinforce data silos (i.e., this department maintains this dataset and no one else can see it), leaders need to tear down these walls and establish new sharing policies.[4] They're also the ones who will establish professional development programs, which can position the system for ultimate success. Schools have had data initiatives before; it is up to the leaders to shape the SLDS as something different and important, not just the next in a series of temporary data initiatives. How the leaders discuss and position the SLDS will greatly impact how the educators see it and use it.

Confidence in the System

To prove its usefulness to teachers and administrators, there must be confidence in the system's output, meaning that high levels of trust in the data and trust in others exist.[5] A strong data quality process and governance will provide assurance in the data and process as a whole, though each user of the system has a responsibility as well. These policies should be shared with each user to promote this understanding and trust in data quality. If the results of reports and data analysis can't be trusted because of poor data quality, what would compel educators to continue to lean on this resource to drive their classroom decisions? A feedback loop is essential to building trust and quality data. In that same vein, there must also be a high level of trust in the community, that the other users and administrators of the system are ensuring the data quality and using the data to achieve a common goal and not to punish or embarrass colleagues unnecessarily.

Redefine Data and Their Uses

Among circles of educators today, data are largely associated with the No Child Left Behind law (NCLB), a measure that is especially unpopular among teachers. NCLB introduced more achievement data and accountability requirements to schools than had ever been seen previously. The huge uptick in standardized tests has given schools more achievement data than ever to interpret, though the law only requires these data be used as a compliance tool. While NCLB does create more data and primes the education system for a shift to a culture of data, in and of itself it doesn't provide the framework for data-driven decisions. Making the leap from data to actionable information is the next big hurdle in bringing the culture of data to the classroom.

Say it loud and say it often: SLDS and related data initiatives are not simply standardized test scores.[6] It is vital that the SLDS project be presented truthfully from the beginning, highlighting how it is new and different. Equally important, administrators must allay teacher concerns about what the data will be used for. SLDSs provide access to rich and varied data for educators. They provide access to more types of data, enabling a move from the NCLB-enforced accountability model to the continuous improvement model.[7] The ability to move beyond standardized test scores and to use the scores to learn about students in a timely fashion provides tools for teachers that have never before been available. From longitudinal data, instructional changes oriented toward increased student achievement become a reality. Using systems like response to intervention to target individuals who need varying levels of assistance (as we discuss in this chapter) and better gauging instructional effectiveness are just a few examples of applications of longitudinal data use for instructional purposes.[8]

Opening up access to data is a key advantage that an SLDS allows, thus enabling use of data that give greater insight into all school employees, even teachers of untested subjects and office administrators. It allows them to use the data, asking questions and receiving answers that could change their teaching and enable higher proficiency among their students. For teachers, this cultural shift in how the data are viewed makes all the difference. Data become an enabler, a job aid, rather than an obligation and a method of judgment. To make effective use of this data resource, teachers must understand what the data represent and the way they will be used, and be ready to use the findings to alter their instructional methods.[9] Administrators are key players in dispelling misconceptions about data use and reinforcing the SLDS's value.

Discuss the Data

Once the SLDS is up and accessible (and hopefully even before), it's essential to talk about the data. Engage in conversations and remind teachers and administrators that the data are there and should be used and not ignored. In mapping out what each user group needs to know, including representatives from each in the planning phase is a best practice.

Teachers know what data they use, and what data they would use if they had access to them, and should thus be consulted during the system design phase. Including them from the beginning will help a new SLDS be less of a shock to the system and more in line with teacher needs.

There are many uses for longitudinal data. And, knowing that educators are neither experts in data analysis nor looking for more job duties, it's important to be clear from the beginning about what the school hopes to accomplish with the data. Creating a shared vocabulary around these functions, and a common understanding, will help each person understand his or her role in the system and the role of data in the school's culture. Setting out the requirements for each user group is an essential planning exercise to ensure that correct access is granted to the system. Ultimately, conversations about data should establish that the focus is here to stay and teacher support and enthusiasm are a vital part of the movement.

Teacher Education and Professional Development

Secretary of Education Arne Duncan has noted repeatedly that in order for our education system's capacity to educate children effectively to improve, "the broadest population of current and future teachers must become data literate."[10] Teacher confidence and preparedness to utilize data in the classroom have been issues of concern among teachers and administrators alike. Several studies have found that teachers' confidence in their data skills affects the likelihood of their using data to make decisions.[11] When thinking about educating today's teachers on data use, leaders find themselves in a quandary. We are faced with a system full of educators with little or no data literacy; providing pre-service training for today's teachers is simply not an option. The march to a more data-literate teacher workforce will inevitably be a slow one. A strong combination of teacher preparation programs including data analysis in their course of study, in-service training and ongoing collaborative working groups can foster this confidence and proficiency in the necessary skills that teachers need to effectively use data in their classroom decision making. Additionally, an ongoing training plan is necessary to truly provide educators with the skills necessary to facilitate the culture shift.

Teacher Preparation Programs

Without a doubt, the programs that train and certify teachers hold a large part of the responsibility for including and emphasizing data-driven decision making as a key strategic tool at the educator's disposal.[12] The knowledge and skills that need to be developed to think logically about data systems, and involve data use in educational activities, are complex and require academic cultivation. However, without the professional knowledge and relevancy, the value of learning these data skills in pre-service training is questionable. It's not until teachers are in the classroom that they will truly be able to put these skills to use in context, so completely relying on pre-service programs to provide this expertise is not feasible. A key element of pedagogical data literacy is being able to put data into context with a vast base of pedagogical knowledge; learning too much about data before the knowledge base of educational methods is built up could be a waste. Some mixture of pre-service and in-service training on data-driven decision-making skills is essential to keeping them germane to the practice of teaching.

It's fair to say that the existing statistics and data analysis education required to receive a teaching license are not sufficient to meet the growing demands on our educational system. To truly rise to the challenges in a data-driven culture, teachers need to be proficient in principles of assessment and statistics, as well as comfortable with the technology used to deliver this functionality.[13] One key reason for this is that this concept is new and iconoclastic for the teaching profession, with many instructors in teacher-prep programs being likewise untrained in data literacy. Having a statistics or math-based training class, similarly, doesn't provide the expertise in education that is needed.[14] To truly shake up the status quo in teacher training, professors need to be trained as well.

Onsite Training for In-Service Teachers

While training at the university level is very important in instilling a respect for and capacity to use data in new teachers, relying solely on institutions of teacher prep is too heavy a burden. Training current in-service teachers with the skills they need to incorporate data into their classroom and educational activities is essential. In training teachers on how to ask, receive and interpret data, an intensive data training session is recommended. This will involve mentoring from a data expert, sample data and a demonstration of analysis. This step is crucial in enabling the SLDS to change the way that education is administered. Teachers are used to, and indeed have been trained to, receive certain data on students. Without education on how to incorporate new and more plentiful data into their day-to-day activities (lesson planning, testing, addressing student needs), there's no reason they won't continue to use the data in the same ways and for the same purposes. Trainers must be brought in to inspire them to break out of the box in which they've operated before and entertain new possibilities. Training sessions should be recurring to encourage ongoing data use and skills enhancement.

To make the training valuable for teachers, using real data is recommended. This can help to paint a clear picture for teachers about how data usage can change outcomes for their students. Rather than a dry, textbook session of theories and definitions, use their classroom data for illustrative purposes. Making concepts hit home is crucial in keeping the skills relevant. True data literacy cannot be achieved until teachers have the opportunity to make data-driven decisions in their own classroom.[15] Additionally, when encouraging educators to incorporate data into their classroom decisions, start by focusing on a few key data indicators. The breadth of data in an SLDS can be overwhelming and starting small can help to ease these feelings and show utility early on.[16]

Collaborative Working Groups

Fostering a collaborative learning environment among teachers is also a best practice. Make no mistake, there is a lot to learn in incorporating a culture of data-driven decisions in the classroom, so creating a group learning experience is a great way to set up the system to succeed.[17] There is a body of research suggesting, according to the U.S. Department of Education's report on teachers using data, that "working with data tends to increase the amount of collaboration among teachers, suggesting that working with data and collaborating on instruction may be mutually reinforcing school improvement practices."[18] These learning communities help to foster higher levels of curiosity, make educators better at spotting and correcting mistakes and generate creativity in using data to enhance classroom decisions and activities.[19] "A comparison of teacher responses during individual and group administration of the data scenarios suggests that teachers are more likely to reach valid conclusions and exhibit a broader range of data literacy concepts and skills when working in small groups," a recent study by the U.S. Department of Education found.[20]

The learning community process mirrors the scientific process taught to students today. These data teams work together on how to improve teaching, examining data together and learning, and sharing findings with colleagues.[21] As time goes on, and the data prove useful in initial instances, administrators and educators will begin to see the possibilities. They'll ask more sophisticated questions, realizing they can get answers that are more specific and targeted than they ever could before.

DATA-DRIVEN DECISION TOOLS

As you can see, there are many leadership-driven changes that facilitate a data-centered culture. There are also some tools that can be utilized to make the use of SLDS efficient and targeted from the beginning and have a major impact on solving some of the biggest, most persistent issues in the modern educational system. How to increase graduation rates, how to provide personalized learning for all students and data usage by educators are all issues where longitudinal data hold promise to change the equation. These tools use longitudinal data and create the opportunity to make a breakthrough in some of the most relevant educational issues of our time. Systems like *response to intervention* and *early warning systems* become even more powerful when associated with up-to-date longitudinal data. A comprehensive and user-friendly interface is essential to stakeholders' ability to understand and contextualize data, and dashboards provide a primary tool for accessing and understanding longitudinal data. These applications also amount to a more proactive use of data rather than a reactive, reflective use of them.

RESPONSE TO INTERVENTION (RTI)

One of the most promising longitudinal data-driven tools to positively impact student outcomes is Response to Intervention (RTI). It is an official process that schools use at the classroom level to systematically identify students' academic and behavioral needs, intervene, and track the responses to those interventions using data. It offers the ability to look at the effects of specific interventions on certain academic or behavioral problems.[22] RTI involves monitoring student progress over time and adjusting methods used depending on the student's response. If a student has a response that is below a certain threshold in respect to her peers, a learning disability might ultimately be diagnosed.[23] Where RTI offers something that traditional models don't is the options in between putting the child into special education and traditional mainstreamed classrooms, including enabling schools to better execute inclusive education.[24]

The rise of RTI as a respected and accepted method of addressing children's special academic and behavioral needs is relatively recent. In October 2001, President George W. Bush established the President's Commission on Excellence in Special Education (PCESE) to tackle issues relating to students with special needs and their education. In July 2002, the PCESE released a report emphasizing the "joint roles of both general and special education in meeting the educational needs of all students."[25] The report also strongly advocated support for prevention and intervention over the "antiquated" prevailing model. Striving to help students early using RTI methods is optimal, while providing special education for "those who do not respond to strong and appropriate instruction and methods provided in general education."[26]

Before RTI began to take hold and gain momentum, the "wait-to-fail" approach was predominant. In this instance, a child might be well below average in a key skill such as learning to read, but still above the qualifications for special education. In that case, the child must continue to stay in a traditional classroom setting with no remediation, and only after he is tested again after a period of time and his scores have worsened enough to place him in special education can he receive it. Time is lost in waiting for the child to qualify for special education, and that time is valuable when we're talking about a key skill like learning to read.[27] Additionally, there were several conflicting definitions of what constitutes a *learning disability* (LD), and it required showing a gap between IQ and achievement. It was difficult to apply before students were in third grade, as they needed to have a certain threshold of curricular content to be tested to calculate IQ and achievement.[28] Misdiagnosing (or overdiagnosing) LDs can cost the state and its special education programs valuable resources; it is important to correctly identify students with special needs and intervene in a timely manner. RTI allows just that.

In response to the PCESE report and recommendations, Congress enacted several key changes to the Individuals with Disabilities Education Act (IDEA) in 2004 (including renaming it the Individuals with Disabilities Education Improvement Act).[29] Under the new guidelines, "the federal government officially allowed students to be classified as learning disabled based on documentation of how well they respond to interventions."[30] Essentially, IDEA allows RTI without mandating it. This update has led to the increased interest in and use of RTI as a method of pinpointing students with varying levels of LDs (including minor LDs that wouldn't qualify for special education), intervening and monitoring the effect of those interventions. The methodology and intellectual framework utilized by RTI has existed since the 1960s and in the past 10 years has gained momentum, largely with the updates to IDEA and the PCESE report. RTI is widely seen as a valid means of officially evaluating children with learning disabilities for entitlement to disability services.[31] Longitudinal data enable this technology to be more efficient, connected to the student record and more up to date.

Any statistician will tell you that more data lead to more accurate results. To that end, RTI offers more longitudinal data and the opportunity for more valid output and ultimately better decisions. With several tiers of testing, intervention and retesting for changed outcomes and positive progress, the opportunity to diagnose, verify and see what's working (and confirm the judgments made in previous tests) is a key advantage of RTI. The risk of mislabeling a child as learning disabled has never been higher and RTI provides a check-and-balance system for this.[32] The most popular and streamlined method of RTI offers a standard protocol for interventions for all students, taking a unified approach to problems like reading level and behavioral issues.

The Standard Protocol Model of RTI takes a three-tiered approach to intervention. At the first level, the entire population of students is tested. The second level involves fewer students, those who would have tested in the borderline or negative zones in the initial tier. Those who respond to interventions in this level will not be tested further, but those who don't improve will progress to the third tier of intervention, most usually special education and individually focused interventions.[33] RTI offers a standard way to identify students' learning problems big and small, tracking interventions, and monitoring progress. "Under normal conditions, these systematic interventions with rigorous progress monitoring would be expected to result in academic growth. In the absence of such academic growth, after several well-documented instructional interventions, a learning disability is assumed to exist under the new RTI procedures."[34]

Using RTI for Personalized Learning

The data from the RTI can then be stored in the SLDS, providing greater context in the future. In the example of a child with delayed reading skills, if a problem manifests with his reading in the future, the educators will know what worked and what did not, making an intervention plan taking that into account. RTI programs offer a substantial increase in data points collected, enabling a more accurate and targeted intervention for students. An SLDS offers the ability to store this information in an accessible, contextualized and usable format to promote better student outcomes and individualized learning.

Like any method of solving a problem, RTI involves several discrete steps with opportunities for students to be tested, problems to be addressed and reevaluation of actions. RTI is unique in that it relies on data, and an SLDS can enhance the ability to efficiently carry out this process. Brown-Chidsey and Steege suggest five steps in the problem-solving sequence of RTI:

1. Problem identification
2. Problem definition

3. Designing intervention plans

4. Implementing the intervention and progress monitoring

5. Problem solution[35]

For each step of RTI, longitudinal data offer greater insight and opportunity to make it a more valuable process. RTI is also an opportunity to use the robust longitudinal data in the SLDS, showcasing the utility of longitudinal data in the execution of an existing and established process, enabling a better education for all students and providing a roadmap for educators to achieve it.

Problem Identification

Identifying that something is amiss in a student's abilities or behaviors is the first step in the RTI process, which entails noting any and all moments when the teacher notices a student's difficulties.[36] Consequently, the problem can be noted by any number of stakeholders in a child's education: teachers, parents, administrators, bus drivers and even students themselves. An SLDS provides a way to catalog these data points. Perhaps each data point on its own might not indicate a problem, but if several people note it, it might indicate something that needs remediation. An SLDS also provides permanence to these data— should a child change schools and when the child moves up a grade, the issues noted along the way can be included to get a more complete picture of what's going on and ensure time is not lost in identifying a problem.

Problem Definition

Taking into account the data points in the identification stage, it will be possible to define the problem. Is the child having difficulty learning to read, or does he have poor eyesight and need glasses? Does he have a behavioral issue that is preventing him from concentrating on his studies? Based on the data collected, a probable definition of the issue at hand can be made. To diagnose a problem, the student's abilities in the area in question will be compared to those of his peers and what is expected of his grade level. Some problems are minor enough that they won't require intervention and remediation, but others of a more severe nature could necessitate intervention to bring the child up to grade level.[37] SLDSs provide a prime means of streamlining the RTI process, documenting incidents and interventions, connecting them to student records and providing this historical information to new teachers to facilitate swift and informed action.[38]

SLDSs, in addition to keeping track of historical data on the student, provide the additional rubric of comparing the student to other students. For instance, it would be possible to use the system to find other students with similar ability levels and see what problem they were diagnosed with. The SLDS, then, can aid in defining and classifying the issues the student is facing and provide history into what works and what doesn't in remediation.

Designing Intervention Plans

Once the problem is identified and defined, the next step in RTI involves putting a specific and prescribed intervention plan in place. In the *problem-solving method*, each issue will correlate to a series of interventions to remedy the problem. If a child is found to be delayed in learning to read, a general plan of interventions, such as alternative teaching plans and other supports, will be charted. With frequent retesting and gauging of the child's response to the interventions, time won't be lost in getting feedback on whether the remediation is having the intended effects.

Since it is a protocol, RTI gives a prescribed next step for interventions for children with similar problems. As we know, simply providing data isn't enough; contextualizing data and giving suggestions on what should be done to remedy problems or potential issues is an important measure to ensure the information is helpful and fully utilized. Longitudinal data can provide this context, showing areas where a student needs improvement and intervention plans that have worked for children with similar issues. The SLDS can provide a forum for tracking and communicating results of the intervention for future educators of the child and of other children with similar issues.

Implementing the Intervention and Monitoring Progress

In the next step, the child's progress is monitored and intervention efforts are recorded. For a reading issue, this could involve cataloging the different approaches and activities that were tried and performing a regular reading fluency test or recording to note changes or progress in the student's abilities. It's essential to know how accurately the intervention protocol was followed, as an incorrect or partial following of the plan won't have the intended results.[39]

So, this step involves monitoring the student's progress, but also the interventions themselves. Perhaps certain interventions are less effective when results are viewed of larger samples of students; those interventions can be adjusted over time. Both of these tasks require data to be tracked, and an SLDS enables that.

Problem Solution

The intervention protocol will set out a certain list of criteria that denotes the problem has been solved. Perhaps the child is now reading at grade level and has mastered prescribed vocabulary and abilities. The final step is to be able to define what success looks like, determining when the intervention should end and how to proceed.

EARLY WARNING SYSTEMS

Early Warning Systems (EWSs) are a functional application that uses longitudinal data to answer important questions, producing alerts when certain conditions are met. It can be logically programmed to target key questions, and, using longitudinal data, is a great way to use data in a timely fashion.

These systems send an alert or assign a risk level to students meeting certain criteria, with the hope that their trajectory could be changed through interventions by educators and they'd still be able to successfully graduate high school. The DQC recommends supporting these EWSs that monitor students' readiness for graduation and career and college readiness as well.

Using EWS: Graduation Rates and Beyond

With the national graduation rate around 75 percent nationally, one in four students will leave high school without a diploma. Whereas the graduation rate has increased (in 2001, it was 72 percent), the number of students leaving school without graduating constitutes a drag on the economy.[40] Employers looking for students with the credentials to work in the knowledge economy are in a bind. Students with no high school diploma have a more difficult time finding a job and earn less over their lifetime. Indeed, society as a whole benefits from a more educated workforce, as it enables more success. The system has struggled with how best to address this problem: when the interventions should be made (and when it is too late), which interventions are effective, and how much funding is necessary. EWSs offer the opportunity for timely intervention and the opportunity to create new conventional wisdom about what causes students to drop out.

With the amounts of longitudinal data available to us, the ability to identify students as early as elementary school who are at risk for not graduating exists, and interventions can change their course.[41] Certain factors can be flagged early to signal a student who might need increased attention from teachers. In high school, three key precursors are seen as the "ABCs" of dropout prediction: attendance, behavior, and course success. Taken together, they're the most accurate predictor of future noncompletion of high school, better than demographics or test scores.[42] We also know that things like a decline in the student's reading and math scores over time, disciplinary problems, being over age for grade and failing ninth grade are among the high school indicators used to identify students at risk.[43] However, it's also accepted that often there's little to be done to change a student's trajectory once she reaches high school. Research and longitudinal data can be used to predict even earlier, when there is still time to change a negative outcome.

If these signs are noted, the issue can be investigated and perhaps remedied in near real time. A trend might be noted where a certain class or population are showing similar signs, which can be corrected as well. With real-time longitudinal data, we don't have to wait for students to drop out (or fail a grade, or even a test) to intervene and make adjustments to their education. Longitudinal data, once certain amounts are reached, can lend themselves to predictive use, and the capacity to proactively use data can impact our educational system's ability to solve the dropout issue.

The Charlotte-Mecklenburg school district in North Carolina has pioneered a system using the district's longitudinal data to track and flag students when they enter Kindergarten based on factors making them at risk for dropping out. An elementary student might be flagged as at risk if he has transferred schools frequently, if his family doesn't speak English at home, or if the child is much younger or much older than his class. This information can affect the education these children receive for the better, changing everything from the teachers to whom they're assigned to which special programs they're enrolled in. Ultimately, the way the school spends its money is dramatically impacted, with a greater ability to measure and prove return on investment in terms of a lower dropout rate.[44]

Beyond the utility of longitudinal data to prevent dropping out from occurring, we also can use the data to encourage graduation and college enrollment. So, instead of just stopping something bad from happening, we can use the same data to determine the factors that college graduates share in their K–12 years and use them to foster those same factors in all students. This sort of activity is beginning in schools like Montgomery County, Maryland's, 144,000-student district, and with a few years' worth of longitudinal data there is a real possibility for states to proactively use their data to encourage college graduation-track achievement in their elementary schoolers.[45] One study investigated what factors make a student ready to take algebra early. Taking algebra early is a factor often associated with academic success and a generally accepted benchmark for students with high potential to go to college. Having the breadth of data that an SLDS contains enables us to figure out what factors lead to success in certain situations, or in this case early success in algebra. Using rich datasets to analyze the students who have done well, we can figure out what factors distinguished them from their peers and ensure that in the future students with similar credentials are pushed into early algebra. An EWS enables these students to be identified and flagged. There are also predictive models that can project what a student's SAT score would be, and thereby which universities would be an option for that student according to their admission criteria and based on the student's eighth-grade marks.

EWSs and predictive modeling are two tools that some states now use with their longitudinal data. To make these predictive analytics accurate enough to be trusted, huge datasets are needed. In an SLDS, having more data points and using as much testing and intervention data as possible decreases the rate of errors and makes the results—the flags given to certain at-risk students—more valid. Being able to change the course of a student at risk for dropping out has huge implications for schools and society as a whole. A higher graduation rate truly benefits everyone—the students who have a high school diploma and the society of which they're productive members. By keeping track of all students and using various factors and many data points, EWSs offer the opportunity to address all students' needs, ensuring that excellent students are appropriately challenged and that students in danger of failing are remediated.

Dealing with Errors

With an EWS, like many of the applications that will use longitudinal data, it's unrealistic to expect 100 percent accuracy from the outputs. Dr. Sean Mulvenon, who works with the University of Arkansas' NORMES system, cautions against expecting perfection from these systems, but, rather, discussing what level of accuracy the institutions are comfortable with.[46] Discuss ways to use data modeling and make use of the data that are available to impact educational decisions.

"If we're nearing the point where we know 95 percent of it is correct, we can model effectively what's going on in those schools," explains Mulvenon. If a classroom of 25 students has a 96 percent accuracy rate, you essentially have 24 of the 25 students spot on. With this accuracy level, you know what's going on in that classroom. "And that's a very meaningful target. But we can spend an inordinate amount of time and money trying to get that twenty-fifth kid correct, and just really break the system in the process." While it's important to place data accuracy as a primary goal, realize that getting all of the data correct all of the time is simply unfeasible, and focusing on that will be to the detriment of the system as a whole.

CONCLUSION

DQC director Aimee R. Guidera sums it up: "Data is the least sexy of all the issues."[47] Though data's solid standing as unexciting and mundane is hardly a point of contention among anyone in the field, it's our view that data are the linchpin that enables our educational systems to rise to the challenges of the knowledge economy, offering mechanisms to improve delivery and results and revolutionizing the way Americans are educated. Sexy or not, data are vital to our education system's future. SLDSs position the education system to make better decisions and provide more effective learning environments for students, if the culture of data supports it. Having the data isn't enough; tools and processes need to be established to enable the data to be understood, contextualized and used to change actions for the data to have any real impact on the issues that our educational system faces and on the culture of data use in our schools. Setting up SLDSs using the tools and processes we've detailed in this chapter sets up each state to move from reactive data use to proactive data use and make real progress toward providing a better education to its students.

NOTES

1. Data for Action 2012, "Focus on People to Change Data Culture" (November 2012), Data Quality Campaign annual report.
2. Amy Wilkinson, interview with author, July 27, 2012.
3. Lane B. Mills, "Creating a Data-Driven Culture: Leadership Matters," SAS white paper, 2009, http://misapps.unx.sas.com/data/cosmos-images/104995_0211.pdf.
4. Ibid.
5. Data Quality Campaign, "What Is Data Literacy and How Do We Achieve It?" July 17, 2012, webinar.
6. Ellen B. Mandinach, Edith S. Gummer, and Robert D. Muller, "The Complexities of Integrating Data-Driven Decision Making into Professional Preparation in Schools of Education: It's Harder Than You Think," report from an Invitational Meeting, May 12, 2011.
7. Ellen B. Mandinach and Sharnell S. Jackson, *Transforming Teaching and Learning through Data-Driven Decision Making* (Thousand Oaks, CA: Corwin, 2012).
8. Institute of Educational Services, "Using Student Achievement Data to Support Instructional Decision Making," IES Practice Guide (2009).
9. Jan Matthews, Susan Trimble, and Anne Gay, "But What Do You Do with the Data?" May 2007, http://www.principals.org/portals/0/content/55501.pdf.
10. Ellen B. Mandinach, Edith S. Gummer, and Robert D. Muller, "The Complexities of Integrating Data-Driven Decision Making into Professional Preparation in Schools of Education."
11. Barbara Means, Eva Chen, Angela DeBarger, and Christine Padilla, "Teachers' Ability to Use Data to Inform Instruction: Challenges and Supports," U.S. Department of Education, Office of Planning, Evaluation and Policy Development, Washington, DC, 2011, http://www2.ed.gov/rschstat/eval/data-to-inform-instruction/report.pdf.
12. Ellen B. Mandinach, Edith S. Gummer, and Robert D. Muller, "The Complexities of Integrating Data-Driven Decision Making into Professional Preparation in Schools of Education."

13. Ellen B. Mandinach and Sharnell S. Jackson, *Transforming Teaching and Learning through Data-Driven Decision Making.*

14. Ibid.

15. Ellen B. Mandinach, Edith S. Gummer, and Robert D. Muller, "The Complexities of Integrating Data-Driven Decision Making into Professional Preparation in Schools of Education."

16. Lane B. Mills, "Creating a Data-Driven Culture."

17. Ellen B. Mandinach, Edith S. Gummer, and Robert D. Muller, "The Complexities of Integrating Data-Driven Decision Making into Professional Preparation in Schools of Education."

18. Barbara Means, Eva Chen, Angela DeBarger, and Christine Padilla, "Teachers' Ability to Use Data to Inform Instruction: Challenges and Supports."

19. Ellen B. Mandinach, Edith S. Gummer, and Robert D. Muller, "The Complexities of Integrating Data-Driven Decision Making into Professional Preparation in Schools of Education."

20. U.S. Department of Education, "Teachers' Ability to Use Data to Inform Instruction."

21. Nancy Love, "Taking Data to New Depths," *National Staff Development Council* 25, no.4 (Fall 2004).

22. Rachel Brown-Chidsey and Mark W. Steege, *Response to Intervention: Principles and Strategies for Effective Practice*, 2nd ed. (New York: Guilford Press, 2010).

23. William N. Bender and Cara Shores, *Response to Intervention: A Practical Guide for Every Teacher* (Thousand Oaks, CA: Corwin Press & Sage Publications, 2007).

24. Rachel Brown-Chidsey and Mark W. Steege. *Response to Intervention: Principles and Strategies for Effective Practice.*

25. Ibid.

26. President's Commission on Excellence in Special Education, "A New Era: Revitalizing Special Education for Children and Their Families," Washington, DC, 2002, http://www2.ed.gov/legislation/FedRegister/other/2002-2/040402c.html (accessed September 26, 2012).

27. Rachel Brown-Chidsey and Mark W. Steege, *Response to Intervention: Principles and Strategies for Effective Practice.*

28. William N. Bender and Cara Shores, *Response to Intervention: A Practical Guide for Every Teacher.*

29. Rachel Brown-Chidsey and Mark W. Steege, *Response to Intervention: Principles and Strategies for Effective Practice.*

30. William N. Bender and Cara Shores, *Response to Intervention: A Practical Guide for Every Teacher.*

31. Ibid.

32. Ibid.

33. Ibid.

34. Ibid.

35. Rachel Brown-Chidsey and Mark W. Steege, *Response to Intervention: Principles and Strategies for Effective Practice.*

36. Ibid.

37. Ibid.

38. William N. Bender and Cara Shores, *Response to Intervention: A Practical Guide for Every Teacher.*

39. Rachel Brown-Chidsey and Mark W. Steege, *Response to Intervention: Principles and Strategies for Effective Practice.*

40. Lindsey Layton, "High School Graduation Rate Rises in U.S.," *Washington Post* (online), March 19, 2012, http://www.washingtonpost.com/local/education/high-school-graduation-rate-rises-in-us/2012/03/16/gIQAxZ9rLS_story.html (accessed November 6, 2012).

41. Aimee Guidera of Data Quality Campaign, "Five Pressing Challenges for Effective Data Use," September 2012, http://www.pie-network.org/buzz/summit-2012/five-pressing-challenges-for-effective-data-use (accessed October 24, 2012).

42. Data Quality Campaign, "Hot Topic: Supporting Early Warning Systems," 2011, http://dataqualitycampaign.org (accessed November 5, 2012).

43. Robert M. Hauser Koenig and Judith Anderson, *High School Dropout, Graduation and Completion Rates: Better Data, Better Measures, Better Decisions* (Washington, DC: National Academies Press, 2011).

44. Michelle R. Davis, "Data Tools Aim to Predict Student Performance," *Education Week*, February 8, 2012, http://www.edweek.org/dd/articles/2012/02/08/02predicting.h05.html (accessed October 25, 2012).

45. Ibid.

46. Jared Knowles, "Early Warning Systems," NCES Conference, Washington, DC, February 13, 2013.

47. Michelle Davis, "Finding Your Way in a Data-Driven World," *Education Week Digital Directions*, January 22, 2008, http://www.edweek.org/dd/articles/2008/01/23/3data.h01.html (accessed November 2, 2012).

CHAPTER **12**

It's Not about
the Data

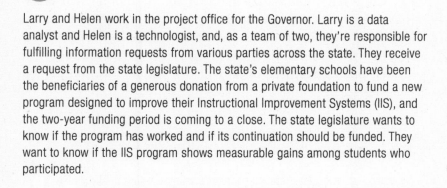

Larry and Helen work in the project office for the Governor. Larry is a data analyst and Helen is a technologist, and, as a team of two, they're responsible for fulfilling information requests from various parties across the state. They receive a request from the state legislature. The state's elementary schools have been the beneficiaries of a generous donation from a private foundation to fund a new program designed to improve their Instructional Improvement Systems (IIS), and the two-year funding period is coming to a close. The state legislature wants to know if the program has worked and if its continuation should be funded. They want to know if the IIS program shows measurable gains among students who participated.

After states have worked tirelessly to implement their SLDS (state-wide longitudinal data system), it might be a surprise to learn all of that effort was not about data. Sure, some of the exercises and process development dealt with data quality and management issues and so on, but the ultimate purpose was not to have better data. The ultimate goal of an SLDS is to impact student outcomes and improve the educational system. Providing data in one central location in a way that is usable to the stakeholders who need it is a catalyst for the type of change the education system needs to make smart improvements and change the equation for today's students.

In the beginning of this book, we gave three examples of data that could aid in smarter decisions relating to policy- and classroom-level problems. With access to an updated, accurate SLDS, the data needed would be easily available and queried, providing timely results to drive decisions. In each example, here's how longitudinal data would have changed the equation.

Using the SLDS, Larry and Helen quickly put together a query to see the past two years' academic growth, the number of elementary-age children receiving remediation or special education, the numbers of children held back a grade and so on, as compared to the growth from the two years prior to the IIS project. These numbers are received, collated and analyzed by Larry and Helen and returned to the state legislators. On the floor of the legislature, elected officials use these numbers to plainly show growth due to the program, thus granting state funding for the program for another two years. Legislators decide to involve the local research university to incorporate additional measures into the IIS for future evaluation. Over the coming two years, progress will continue to be monitored, with the understanding that lack of growth will signal a discontinuation of the funding.

In the same state, at Ashley Elementary, John is a new student in Mrs. Fraser's third-grade class. He is reading below grade level and Mrs. Fraser wants to help him. She is curious as to what John's previous schools have tried to remediate his needs. She needs this information quickly, so time isn't lost in addressing John's pressing need. Before he's compelled to repeat third grade or gets pushed into alternative education, Mrs. Fraser is anxious to pick up where previous teachers have left off to improve John's reading.

During recess, Mrs. Fraser logs into the SLDS and views John's academic record. She notes that earlier in the year, his previous teacher tried several of the recognized interventions for John's age. She sees a full list of remediations to try before he is officially sent to the school's reading specialist and is able to go through the next test with him the next day. She will log the results of her evaluation with him into the SLDS for future reference.

The governor wants to begin a task force to reduce the number of high school dropouts in the state. She asks the state's Department of Education to supply the following information to provide the backbone for an early warning system that alerts educators when kids show certain characteristics. What are the characteristics of high school dropouts? Are there early predictors schools could find in elementary or middle school to better identify at-risk individuals? Do these predictors change in different geographic areas or among different demographic populations?

The Department of Education supplies the task force with several cohorts of longitudinal data, giving the ability to see trends in the academic trajectories of those who did not graduate from high school. The task force works with data scientists to determine these factors and build and test an early warning system on existing data. Eventually, this early warning system will enable educators to receive red-flag warnings for students who are at risk of dropping out and remediate their needs, ultimately lowering the state dropout rate.

Each of these examples is tremendously impacted by the availability and access to longitudinal data. They are examples of how the data within an SLDS aid far-reaching and smarter decisions. The ability to quickly receive accurate answers that impact funding, policy and even an individual student's education are not simply benefits of an SLDS, they're essential to the efficient functioning of the state's educational system. With an SLDS, good intentions and hunches are things of the past. You now have powerful, relevant data at your fingertips to make proactive decisions that impact student learning and success.

WAYS TO SUSTAIN THE SYSTEM

After the SLDS is established, it might feel a little like everyone is just looking at each other, thinking "What now?" You might be curious how you keep the momentum going on the system to ensure the continued return on the investment made through grant dollars and time and energy. You want to make sure the promises upon which the system was developed come to fruition.

SLDSs offer a unique opportunity to improve the country's educational system. We're talking about a game-changing technological advance that would enable educators to make a greater impact on students, allow administrators to more effectively manage and reward teachers and allow states to have a clear picture of what is happening in their educational system. There are many reasons to implement an SLDS, very few good ones to resist it and a whole host of practical decisions and issues to address in the process.

Creating an SLDS is a challenge involving collaboration and political forces and challenges in data management and it will likely span many years. To say it's an arduous task is an understatement. There are many challenges in setting up an SLDS; funding, buy-in from stakeholders, establishing the software and hardware needs and requirements for the system and the rules that govern its functioning are all important and time-consuming prerequisites for getting a system up and running. If your SLDS is properly established, it can quickly show its utility by providing real-time answers that affect policy decisions and educational outcomes.

Many states come at this task because they've been awarded grant money to establish it. Once the system is up and running, once the data are being employed in educational decisions, its value should become apparent and the community investment in it can become self-sustaining. This is the goal: to achieve high levels of community buy-in to the SLDS. It is important to keep the project relevant, work with leaders and allies to build consensus and use the system to promote change and accountability in the educational system. In the end, the goal is for stakeholders to wonder how they ever did their jobs without this resource.

The key ways to sustain the system for continued success and impact, as pictured in Figure 12.1, are to focus on strong leadership,

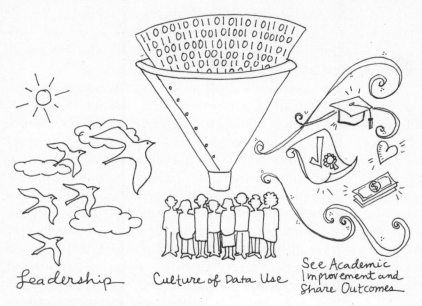

Figure 12.1 Ways to Sustain the SLDS

a culture of data use and the student outcomes and successes of the system.

Leadership

Ultimately, if your state's SLDS is to be implemented and used successfully, there needs to be buy-in and support from every level of your state's educational system. A major change like this demands strong leadership that clearly communicates the system's progress and goals and heralds data use successes. An innovative technology that is accepted grudgingly will quickly become incorporated into the same way things were done, squashing the potential positive changes that innovation might have enabled. For an SLDS, if the longitudinal data aren't used by teachers and administrators to influence their teaching and practice, or if they are used in the same way the current data are used, the SLDS won't enable a shift to a new culture of data. "If there is no consensus among concerned people that following the new methods leads to the desired outcomes any better than the old methods, they are unlikely to behave differently after being trained in the use of new measurement systems or standard operating procedures," says Clayton M. Christensen in *Disrupting Class: How Innovation Will Change the Way the World Learns.*[1]

Leaders should seek to use the power they have in productive ways. As with methods of government, there are several ways of effecting a radical change (think: dictatorship, democracy, and so on). While we certainly wouldn't recommend a dictatorship, a democracy isn't always the best-equipped way for a cultural, disruptive shift in the way business is done.[2] There may be some hard decisions that come from the top that are in the best interest of the system. In the school system, there are many competing interests and audiences, each with a vested interest in preserving the status quo. By its very nature, an SLDS challenges the status quo by providing real-time data on the way things are done, and potentially, a real-time report that the way things are done currently is ineffective. The self-preservation instinct is strong, and sometimes leaders must use their power to overcome these interests and stay on course to SLDS implementation and use.

Governance also has an important leadership role to play in the SLDS. Most SLSDs don't start out with automatic excitement, or even buy-in, from all stakeholders, and Governance will collaborate to take a smart approach to accommodating needs and encouraging acceptance in the early days of the project. Governance is key for states in the design and implementing of a system that works for everyone. When establishing the committee, the group of subject matter experts and concerned parties, keep in mind existing collaborative groups that could be utilized. Creating Governance and SLDS committees might not necessitate a completely separate group, but rather a reimagining of a previous working group.

As the system grows and is eventually implemented, Governance can transition to be roving advocates for the system within their functional roles, encouraging their colleagues to use the data and alerting the Governance group to usage issues. They can bring up possible areas for the SLDS to improve or expand to, and also have a clear picture of what is possible and how to achieve it. The members of the Governance body are assets to the SLDS.

Another key function of the leadership of the SLDS, both in the development phase and after its implementation, is communication. It's vital that the SLDS be portrayed accurately, conveying clearly what the system can and cannot do. While it would be nice to make it the answer to all problems, realistically, it won't be perfect. Realistic expectations should be set during all phases of the project; throughout the planning and implementation share updates on the progress. And definitely ensure that the SLDS is given credit whenever new data connections can be made that impact major educational initiatives (such as in the previous examples).

Strong communication surrounding the SLDS enables a shared way to understand the problem and solution.[3] If everyone understands the issue and the remedy in the same way, this makes the solution logical to all and stakeholder agreement higher. This tactic requires strong communication from leaders to stakeholders and an open discourse regarding the solution. SLDS projects will involve winning the hearts and minds of a variety of stakeholding groups, which is necessary for its ultimate success and continued usefulness. "Teachers, taxpayers, administrators, parents, students and politicians have divergent priorities and disagree strongly about how to improve," Christensen says.[4] Common-language framing of the issue can enable more effective use of other tools, like strategic planning, measurement systems and salesmanship.

Culture of Data Use

As fundamental as it is to say, the more data are used, the more they will be valued. Showing and, for some stakeholders, experiencing them firsthand will prove their value. This sort of experience proves the value of the data and makes for higher levels of buy-in among stakeholders. Teachers can begin to see the value of having longitudinal data on their students, see how the data shape their instructional methods to make them more effective and see improvements in tracked data for their students. Administrators can see the new automated procedures in reporting and managing teachers' results. An SLDS comes, often, at a high cost and takes many hours of energy and effort from stakeholders. Once it becomes apparent that the end result is solidly worth it, it will ultimately generate more enthusiasm.

Additionally, use of the data can change the community feeling about the data. For instance, if a teacher uses data from the SLDS to influence a classroom-level decision (like Mrs. Fraser addressing John's reading issues), she not only will be more likely to visit the SLDS again when another academic challenge arises, but will be inclined to update the system with data she's found. And, beyond that, data users will be more likely to contribute their suggestions or flag system issues as they're found. Every positive interaction with the SLDS improves its standing among stakeholders, reinforcing the culture of data at all levels.

See Academic Improvement and Share Outcomes

The education system faces many important issues today. Topping most lists of the most urgent problems in education are teacher effectiveness and increasing the number of students who graduate with the skills they need to succeed in college and a career.[5] As we've noted in this book, SLDSs hold promise in gaining new insights into these issues and opportunities to solve these difficult and complex problems.

The SLDS can easily prove its worth by supplying answers that are being widely sought. In the example of the governor's task force for targeting the high school dropout rate, the SLDS supplied data that enabled the early warning system that eventually led to a decrease in the dropout rate; longitudinal data's role in this solution should be celebrated. By all means, when the news is shared that the state's graduation rate is up, tell the public why. Tell the public that this shared community resource has positively impacted its students and its future workforce is smarter because of it. These sorts of success stories should be publicized, as they'll increase the public's understanding of what the system is and what it can do. If funding for the SLDS ever goes into jeopardy, greater public support and awareness of the system helps.

And beyond the big-news stories like that one, it's also important to keep an eye on what the system does locally. Share stories about how access to longitudinal data impacted one school for the better, or even one student's outcomes. Ultimately, the SLDS isn't a secret project that the public doesn't care about. It is a public resource, and we encourage wide discussion and touting of successes.

Another key educational issue that the SLDS can positively impact is teacher effectiveness. As we've discussed, there are many opportunities to use data from the SLDS to evaluate teachers. Going beyond using student achievement data is a key benefit of these systems, and one that we hope will give rich insights into what makes a great teacher great, and how good teachers can be made great. By showing that data can be used to reward and reinforce good behavior and not to punish poor teachers, SLDSs can improve their standing among educators. Sharing outcomes with the public, especially parents who are very concerned about teacher quality, reinforces the value of the SLDS to these stakeholders as well.

SLDSs also pose an opportunity to move beyond standardized tests in the measuring of academic achievement and improvement. In terms of evaluating teachers, students and schools themselves, involving much more data gives a clearer picture of achievement, presenting a more robust picture of what it means to succeed and grow, because, even though tested knowledge is important, it misses the end result of education, which is producing well-trained and knowledgeable graduates.

CONCLUSION

Over the years spent developing the SLDS, stakeholders and users of the longitudinal data should come to view the system as a community resource. It should be seen as a way to improve the educational system, providing backing for data-driven and logical decisions from educators, administrators, legislators and parents. It's a tool to promote smarter change within the system and accountability of stakeholders across the board. It is vital that states that establish an SLDS continue to give attention to the sustainability of the system by keeping strong leadership and governance involved in promoting and maintaining the system. They must continue their investment in the culture of data at all levels of the educational system and focusing on the positive impacts that the longitudinal data enable at the student level.

Ultimately, it's not about data. It's about people. It's about students, educational improvement and the fact that having an educated society full of taxpayers is more enriching to the society as a whole. It's about better utilizing the scant resources available to the state educational system and making sure what we're doing is working. It's about increasing data security and providing authorized access to those who are entitled to it. It's about accountability. SLDS, at its best, is a means to an end. It offers the American educational system an opportunity to employ modern technology and standards to usher in a new era of excellence—and our kids deserve it.

NOTES

1. Clayton Christensen, Curtis W. Johnson, and Michael B. Horn, *Disrupting Class, Expanded Edition: How Disruptive Innovation Will Change the Way the World Learns* (New York: McGraw-Hill, 2010).
2. Ibid.
3. Ibid.
4. Ibid.
5. Data Quality Campaign, "Data for Action: Focus on People to Change Data Culture," November 2012, http://dataqualitycampaign.org/files/DFA2012%20Annual%20 Report.pdf.

About the Authors

Jamie McQuiggan is a technical writer specializing in education topics at SAS Institute. She has a master's degree in technical communication and experience in software documentation, grant writing and social media strategy. She is a former information developer at IBM and business analyst with Fidelity Investments.

Armistead W. Sapp III is the senior vice president of research and development (R&D) at SAS and is responsible for the development of the software used at more than 65,000 sites in more than 135 countries. As head of the P20 efforts at SAS, Sapp leverages corporate R&D to bring innovative solutions for administration and instruction to the education market. This includes responsibility for SAS Curriculum Pathways, a no-cost Web-based curriculum for middle school and high school. His 20-plus-year career at SAS has encompassed many roles in marketing and R&D, and he was the president of SouthPeak Interactive (a developer and publisher of interactive entertainment software). He is also a contract researcher at Duke University Health System, working on neonatal best practices and safety.

Index

academia
  about, 114–115
  data scientists, 115–117
  establishing protocols for data
    access, 117–118
academic improvement,
  sustainability and, 192–193
administrators
  about, 134–135
  encouraging or requiring data
    use, 135
  evaluating teachers using
    longitudinal data, 135–136
agility, in data management, 60
America COMPETES Act (2007),
  3, 21, 41
American Recovery and
  Reinvestment Act (2009),
  3, 21–22
Annual Professional performance
  Review (APPR), 137–139
answers, getting timely, 5–6
archiving, in metadata
  management, 68

Basch, Charles, 154–155
big data, 115
blurring, of personally
  identifiable information 43
Brown-Chidsey, Rachel,
  174–175
budget, sustainability and, 51
Bush, George W., 172

career ready initiative, in
  Michigan, 92–94
CEDARS, 99
CEDS (Common Education Data
  Standards), 8, 20, 39–40,
  153, 156
Center for Educational
  Performance and
  Information (CEPI), 85–86
centralized data warehouse
  (CDW), 29, 70–71
CFS (Common Follow-Up
  System), 96, 99
Charlotte-Mecklenburg school
  district, 178–179
Christensen, Clayton M.
  *Disrupting Class: How Innovation
  Will Change the Way the World
  Learns*, 190–191
classrooms
  See schools and classrooms
collaboration
  collaborative working groups,
    170–171
  increased, 8
  in teacher-student record
    link, 141
collective impact
  about, 148–149
  facilitating initiatives, 157–160
"Collective Impact" (Kramer
  and Kania), 148–149,
  157–158

college ready initiative, in
    Michigan, 92–94
common data dictionary, 47
Common Education Data
    Standards (CEDS), 8, 20,
    39–40, 153, 156
Common Follow-Up System
    (CFS), 96, 99
communication
    leadership and, 191
    sustainability and, 51–52
confidence in the system, for
    creating a culture of data, 166
connections, new, 8
context, of metadata
    management, 67–68
Core Techniques and
    Technologies for Advancing
    Big Data Science and
    Engineering (BIGDATA), 115
Culatta, Richard, 10
culture of data
    as barrier to success of SLDS,
    27–28
    creating a, 164–171, 191–192
Cuomo, Andrew, 137

data
    See also longitudinal data
    addressing interoperability of,
        38–41
    'big data,' 115
    discussing, 167–168
    encouraging or requiring use
        of by administrators, 135
    privacy and security of, 48
    redefining, 166–167
    security of, 41–45
    siloed, 2
data access
    establishing protocols for,
        117–118
    by parents, 120–122

data collection and integration,
    as barrier to success of
    SLDS, 27
data dictionary, 40, 47
data governance, 36–37
    See also Governance
Data Governance Boards
    establishing, 35–37
    for Florida, 83
data governance committee, 12
data management
    See also metadata management
    about, 57–60
    agility in, 60
    data redundancy in, 59
    incorporating principles of into
        SLDS, 60–75
data management, models for,
    28–30
"data mart," 87
data model, 40
data quality
    Florida case study, 80–81
    MDM (master data
        management), 62–64
Data Quality Campaign, 3
data redundancy, in data
    management, 59
data scientists, 115–117
data standards, 38–40
data stewards, 74–75
data system architecture
    about, 69–70
    centralized data warehouse,
        29, 70–71
    federated data system, 29–30,
        71–73
data-driven decisions, 6–7, 171
designing
    intervention plans as step in
        RTI, 176
    MDM (master data
        management), 64

Disabilities Education Act (IDEA) (2004), 173
Disrupting Class: How Innovation Will Change the Way the World Learns (Christensen), 190–191
DOC-LEAD, 97
dropout, 7
Duncan, Arne, 22, 122–123, 137, 168

Early Childhood Challenge Grant (ECCG), 97
Early Warning Systems (EWSs)
  about, 6, 171, 177
  dealing with errors, 180
  using, 177–180
education
  measuring effectiveness of, 8–9
  for teachers, 168
educational research, improving, 113–114
Educational Technical Assistance Act (2002), 23
effectiveness, of teachers and objectives, 140
efficiency, in data management, 60
evaluating
  current systems, 45–50
  MDM (master data management), 73
  teachers using longitudinal data, 135–136
EWSs (Early Warning Systems)
  about, 6, 171, 177
  dealing with errors, 180
  using, 177–180

Family Educational Record Privacy Act (FERPA, 1974), 26, 41–42, 107, 109–110, 153, 156

Family Policy Compliance Office (FPCO), 113
federal grants, renovating Florida's system with, 79–83
federated data system, 29–30, 71–73
feedback, 123–124
Florida case study
  about, 77–78
  creating a formal Data Governance Body, 83
  data quality, 80–81
  renovating existing system using federal grants, 79–83
  researcher access process, 82
  SLDS (statewide longitudinal data system), 78–79
  unique identifier system, 81–82
Forum of Youth Investment, 150
FPCO (Family Policy Compliance Office), 113
funding
  as barrier to success of SLDS, 26
  for OST programs, 151
fuzzy-match systems, 48

Gates Foundation, 136–137, 139
getting started
  about, 33–34
  addressing interoperability of data, 38–41
  establishing a Data Governance Board, 35–37
  evaluating current systems, 45–50
  planning and preparation, 35
  setting policies for data security and student privacy, 41–45
  sustainability, 50–53

Governance
  first steps for, 37
  importance of , 36–37
  importance of data quality
    and, 62–64
  leadership and, 190
Granholm, Jennifer, 93
Guidera, Aimee, 17

Hawes, Michael, 43
health-care data
  See also out-of-school time
    (OST)
  About, 153–155
  FERPA compliance, 156
Healthy Schools Campaign, 153
Herman, Joan, 133
HIPAA (Health Insurance
  Portability and
  Accountability Act), 26–27,
  153, 156
Hopper, Steven, 100, 101, 103,
  104
Howell, Tom, 85–86, 86–87,
  90, 91

IDEA (Disabilities Education Act,
  2004), 173
implementing
  intervention as step in RTI,
    176–177
  MDM (master data
    management), 64
  metadata management, 68–69
information landscape, 44
Institute of Education Sciences
  (IES), 20, 23, 123
Institutes of Higher Education
  Feedback Report, 99
instructional decision making,
  132–133
Instructional Improvement
  Systems (IIS), 1, 105

interoperability, of metadata
  management, 67–68
invaluable nature of system,
  sustainability and, 52
inventory, of current systems,
  49–50

Kania, John
  "Collective Impact," 148–149,
    157–158
Kovacs, Gene, 78, 79–80, 84n1
Kramer, Mark
  "Collective Impact," 148–149,
    157–158

leadership
  communication and, 191
  for creating a culture of data,
    164–166
  Governance and, 190
  implementing and improving,
    12–13
  for sustainability, 189–191
learning disability (LD), 173
"linchpin," 139
linkage, reinforcing mutual
  benefit from, 46–47
local educational agencies
  (LEAs), 7
longitudinal data
  See also data
  about, 185–187
  administrators evaluating
    teachers using, 135–136
  enabling use of, 109–110
  history of systems, 18–23
  users of, 110–111

Mandinach, Ellen, 132
master data, defined, 58–59
master data management
  (MDM), 58, 60–75
McGroarty, Mike, 68

memorandum of understanding (MOU), 48, 100–101
metadata management
  See also data management
  About, 64–67
  benefits of, 67–69
  implementing, 68–69
Michigan case study
  About, 85–86
  career and college ready initiative, 92–94
  SLDS (statewide longitudinal data system), 86–92
Michigan Consortium for Educational Research (MCER), 93
Michigan Merit Curriculum, 93
Michigan Promise Scholarship (MPS), 93
monitoring
  MDM (master data management), 73
  progress, as step in RTI, 176–177
Montgomery County, Maryland, 179
MOU (memorandum of understanding), 48, 100–101
Mulvenon, Sean, 115, 180

National Assessment for Educational Progress (NAEP), 19
National Center for Education Statistics (NCES), 20
National Council for the Accreditation of Teacher Education (NCATE) Blue Ribbon Panel, 130
National Longitudinal Studies, 19
NC Independent Colleges and Universities (NCICU), 96–98
New York State Education Department (NYSED), 137

No Child Left Behind Act (2001), 3, 20–21, 166–167
NORMES system, 180
North Carolina case study
  about, 95–96
  history, 98–101
  P20W System, 96–101
  Stakeholders, 96–101
  state legislation reinforcing SLDS, 102–104
  vision, 101–102
North Carolina Community Colleges System (NCCCS), 96–104
North Carolina Department of Public Instruction (NCDPI), 113
North Carolina Division of Motor Vehicles (NCDMV), 97
North Carolina Education Research Data Center (NCERDC), 113
North Carolina General Assembly (NCGA), 102

objectives, defining effectiveness of, 140
online analytical processing (OLAP) cubes, 82, 87
onsite training for in-service teachers, 169–170
OST
  See out-of-school time (OST)
outcomes, sharing, for sustainability, 192–193
out-of-school time (OST)
  See also health-care data
  about, 145–148
  collective impact, 148–149
  facilitating collective impact initiatives, 157–160
  what happens during, 149–153

P20 Council, 89–90
P20 system
  about, 152–153
  in Michigan case study, 87
  planning and implementing, 89
P20W (preschool-through-school-
  college-and-workforce),
  45–46, 96–101
parents
  about, 118–119
  data access by, 120–122
  goals of increased access for,
    121–122
  as stakeholders in student
    outcomes, 119–120
PCESE (President's Commission
  on Excellence in Special
  Education), 172
pedagogical data literacy,
  132–133, 169
personalized learning, using RTI
  for, 174–177
personally identifying
  information (PII), 41
perturbation, of personally
  identifiable information, 43
Pittman, Karen, 150, 159–160
planning
  MDM (master data
    management), 61–62
  for SLDS (statewide
    longitudinal data system), 35
policy makers, 109–111
politics, as barrier to success of
  SLDS, 26
Pond, Karl, 96–102
preschool-through-school-
  college-and-workforce
  (P20W), 45–46, 96–101
preserving, in metadata
  management, 68
President's Commission on
  Excellence in Special
  Education (PCESE), 172

privacy, of data, 48
Privacy Technical Assistance
  Center (PTAC), 110, 156
problem definition, as step in
  RTI, 175–176
problem identification, as step in
  RTI, 175
problem solution, as step in
  RTI, 177
problem solving
  about, 163–164
  creating cultures of data,
    164–171
  data-driven decision tools, 171
  Early Warning Systems
    (EWSs), 177–180
  methods of, 176
  response to intervention (RTI),
    172–177
processes, implementing and
  improving, 9–11
professional development, of
  teachers, 168
program assessment, 111
PTAC (Privacy Technical
  Assistance Center),
  110, 156
public information sharing,
  108–109

questions, asking, 5–6

Race to the Top program, 3,
  22, 137
Ready by 21 (RB21)
  initiative, 150
record matching, 48
redefining data and uses, for
  creating a culture of data,
  166–167
regulatory history, 20–23
reporting, accurate and
  effective, 7
research agenda, 112–113

researcher access process, 82
researchers
 about, 112
 improving educational
  research, 113–114
 research agenda, 112–113
Response to Intervention (RTI),
 6, 171, 172–174
retrievability, in metadata
 management, 67
Rhee, Michelle, 122
Rodriguez, Baron, 110, 156
role-based access, to student
 information, 44–45

scalability, as barrier to success of
 SLDS, 27
schools and classrooms
 about, 127–128
 administrators, 134–136
 teachers, 128–134
 teacher-student record link,
  136–141
School-to-Work Opportunities
 Act (STWOA), 20
security
 as barrier to success of SLDS,
  26–27
 of data, 48
SFSF (State Fiscal Stabilization
 Funds), 22
sharing information
 about, 105–107
 academia, 114–118
 parents, 118–122
 policy makers and state-level
  decision makers,109–111
 public, 108–109
 researchers, 112–114
 students, 122–124
siloed data, 2
single view, 59
SLDS (statewide longitudinal
 data system)

About, 2–4, 185–187
challenges to success of,
 25–28
features of, 4–9
Florida, 78–79
Grant Program, 23
implementing and improving,
 9–13
Michigan, 86–92
today's state of, 23–28
Sneaker Net systems, 4–9,
 99–100
stakeholders
 in Michigan, 88–90
 in North Carolina, 96–101
 parents as in student
  outcomes, 119–120
Stanford Social Innovation Review,
 148–149
State Fiscal Stabilization Funds
 (SFSF), 22
state support, sustainability and,
 51–52
state-level decision makers,
 109–111
statewide longitudinal data
 system
 See SLDS (statewide
  longitudinal data system)
Steege, Mark W., 174–175
Strive Network, 158
student privacy, setting policies
 for, 41–45
student unique identifier
 See UID (unique identifier)
students, sharing information
 with, 122–124
STWOA (School-to-Work
 Opportunities Act), 20
support, maintaining,
 sustainability and,
 51–52
suppression, of personally
 identifiable information, 43

sustainability
about, 188–189
academic improvement and,
192–193
budget and, 51
communication and, 51–52
culture of data use, 191–192
invaluable nature of system
and, 52
leadership and, 52, 189–191
sharing outcomes for, 192–193
of SLDS, 50–53
state support and, 51–52
support, maintaining, and,
51–52
system confidence, for creating a
culture of data, 166
system impact, of metadata
management, 68

teacher UID, 140
teachers
about, 128–129
administrators evaluating,
135–136
asking the right questions,
129–130
defining effectiveness of, 140
educating, 168
improving classroom practice
with information, 133–134
interpreting and
contextualizing results,
131–132

onsite training for in-service,
169–170
seeking answers, 130–131
teacher preparation
programs, 169
teacher-student record link
about, 136–137
best practices, 139–141
case study (New York),
137–139
importance of, 139
technology, implementing and
improving, 11–12
triangulation method, 131
Tucker, Bill, 121

UID (unique identifier), 4, 28,
40–41, 81–82, 140
United States Department of
Education, 19–20
University of North
Carolina system (UNC),
96–101

vision, in North Carolina case
study, 101–102
voluntary partnerships,
48–49

Wage Record Interchange System
(WRIS), 46
Wayman, Jeff, 132–133
Williams, Saundra, 100, 102,
103–104